Other Kaplan Books Related to Health Care

Careers in Nursing

NCLEX-RN

Other Books in the Kaplan Higher Education Career Series

Your Bright Future in Business Administration

Your Bright Future in Information Technology

Your Bright Future in Health Care

By Mary K. Kouri

Kaplan Higher Education

Simon & Schuster

NEW YORK · LONDON · SINGAPORE · SYDNEY · TORONTO

Kaplan Publishing
Published by Simon & Schuster
1230 Avenue of the Americas
New York, NY 10020

Copyright 2002 by Kaplan Publishing

All rights reserved. No part of this book may be reproduced or transmitted in any form or by any means, electronic or mechanical, including photocopying, recording, or by any information storage and retrieval system, without the written permission of the Publisher, except where permitted by law.

For bulk sales to schools, colleges, and universities, please contact: Order Department, Simon and Schuster, 100 Front Street, Riverside, NJ 08075. Phone: (800) 223-2336. Fax: (800) 943-9831.

Kaplan® is a registered trademark of Kaplan, Inc.

Contributing Editors: Tanya Burden-Mercer and Dick Dormuth
Editor: Ruth Baygell
Cover Design: Cheung Tai
Production Editor: Maude Spekes
Production Manager: Michael Shevlin
Editorial Coordinator: Déa Alessandro
Executive Editor: Del Franz

Special thanks to Grace Freedson's Publishing Network, LLC.

Note: Dozens of websites have been mentioned in this book for your convenience. It is possible that these sites may contain inaccurate, outdated, or objectionable material. Please be aware that the author, editors, and publisher of this book cannot vouch for the accuracy or integrity of these sites or any information contained therein.

Manufactured in the United States of America
Published simultaneously in Canada

September 2002

10 9 8 7 6 5 4 3 2 1

ISBN: 0-7432-3060-4

TABLE OF CONTENTS

Introduction 1

Chapter 1: An Overview of the Health Care Industry 9

Chapter 2: Working in Health Care 17

Chapter 3: Career Close-Ups 39

Chapter 4: Preparing for Your Career 81

Chapter 5: Paying for Your Education 91

Chapter 6: Moving Ahead 111

Kaplan Higher Education 115

ABOUT THE AUTHOR

Mary K. Kouri is an award-winning writer. She is the author of *Keys to Survival for Caregivers; Keys to Dealing with the Loss of a Loved One;* and *Volunteerism and Older Adults.* Her health writing includes articles on personal health for consumer publications, and newsletters for women's health center managers in hospitals. Ms. Kouri has an M.P.H. in health education and a Ph.D. in adult development psychology. She lives in Centennial, Colorado.

INTRODUCTION

Take just about any job: You'll find someone who loves it and someone who hates it. The explanation isn't in the job or in the person. It's in the match between the work and the worker's skills and preferences. When there's a close match, you'll find a happy worker, a happy boss, and satisfied customers—or in health care, satisfied patients and clients.

The first step in building a career that makes you happy, and in selecting the best health care job for you, is to pinpoint your skills and work preferences. The exercises below help you to do that.

SELF-ASSESSMENT: FINDING THE RIGHT JOB

Richard Nelson Bolles, the "grandfather" of job search techniques, has divided the thousands of job-related skills into three categories. While every job involves skills from each category, many draw heavily on one or two categories.

1. Skills with people of various ages, cultures, backgrounds, needs, and interests
2. Skills with information or data, including knowledge, ideas, facts, figures, statistics
3. Skills with things, including instruments, tools, machines, equipment, vehicles, phones, computers, and other physical objects

When given a choice, which category do you enjoy using most? People, information/data, or things? Which is your second pick? And third?

Introduction

Now let's go a bit further with the self-assessment. On each list, choose ratings of 4 or 3 for items that *best* describe you, and ratings of 2 or 1 for items that *least* describe you. Have fun! There's no wrong answer—except if you lie to yourself.

Part 1: Personality Traits (Who Am I?)

Trait	4	3	2	1
1. Accurate				
2. Analytical				
3. Attentive to detail				
4. Calm				
5. Careful				
6. Cheerful				
7. Compassionate				
8. Considerate				
9. Cooperative				
10. Curious				
11. Dependable				
12. Efficient				
13. Flexible				
14. Friendly				
15. Gentle				
16. Hard-working				
17. Organized				
18. Patient				
19. Punctual				
20. Self-confident				
21. Tactful				
22. Thorough				
23. Tolerant				

Part 2: Skill Choices (Which Competencies Do I Like to Use?)

Skill	4	3	2	1
1. Anticipate needs of others				
2. Communicate in groups				
3. Communicate one-to-one				
4. Communicate by phone				
5. Communicate in writing				
6. Concentrate amid chaos				
7. Cope with interruptions				
8. Follow instruction				
9. Get along with people				
10. Learn by listening				
11. Learn by observing				
12. Learn by reading				
13. Listen attentively				
14. Nurture people				
15. Observe behavior changes				
16. Organize objects (e.g., supplies, work equipment)				
17. Organize tasks and schedules				
18. Repair machines and other objects				
19. Research facts and figures				
20. Teach adults				
21. Teach children				
22. Type fast and accurately				
23. Work with technical data				
24. Work with numbers				

Introduction

Certain personality traits are important to health care workers in general. For example, you need some degree of compassion whether you work at the patient's bedside or answer the phone in a dental office. Punctuality is critical as well. With budget cuts and labor shortages, most organizations can barely hire enough staff to handle the day's work, let alone cover for somebody who's late.

> **WORD TO THE WISE**
>
> While you may shine in a certain skill, you might not enjoy using it *all* the time. Avoid the trap of taking a job that requires heavy use of a skill, or set of skills you don't like—even if people say you're a natural at it!

Beyond the generalities, people succeed in particular occupations because they bring traits and skills the work requires. In turn, they feel satisfied with what the work offers. You'll get a better feel for this when you get to chapter 3. In that chapter, each career close-up features a profile of personality traits and skills, as well as job settings that might pertain to the occupation.

A suitable candidate for an occupation would rate the important skills and personality traits at 4 or 3. For instance, a pharmacy technician needs at least a rating of 3, and preferably 4, on trait #3, attentive to detail. A pharmacy technician should also give a 4 or 3 rating to skill #23, work with technical data.

If you rate yourself as a 3 on traits and skills that are important for an occupation you're considering, you'll probably do fine with that occupation. Just be aware that you might need to strengthen some of your 3-rated traits or skills. For example, if you choose health information technology and give a 3 rating to skill #22, "type fast and accurately," you could upgrade your performance with a little practice.

We'll take a look at those 1 and 2 ratings in a minute. But first, let's pull an example from the real world. Remember when we talked about the match between the worker and the job? Surely you deal with people every now and then who lead you to think, "They're in the wrong job!" You're probably right—they're ill suited in personality, skills, or both. Perhaps they don't like to use the traits and skills the job requires, or they simply don't have them.

As for your 2 and 1 ratings: They might point to areas outside of your strengths or preferences. Or they could indicate traits or skills you really wouldn't want to use on the job.

Let's say you rate yourself as a 2 on trait #6, "cheerful." If you aspire to be a medical assistant, you would have to learn how to maintain a cheerful disposition because the work involves constant interaction with people and periods of high stress. If you'd rather not develop that trait, you might do better in a health care billing office or some other job where you could have minimal contact with people.

Introduction

So as you review trait and skill ratings, ask yourself two questions:
- Do I have it?
- Do I like to use it?

Part 3: Job Setting (Which Work Conditions Suit Me?)

Understand that health occupations "live" in any number of work settings. As a registered nurse, you might work in a hospital emergency room or an insurance company, in a doctor's office or a school system, just for openers. So imagine the job settings as different kinds of soil where you might or might not flourish.

Condition	4	3	2	1
1. Business side of health care				
2. Clear-cut job description				
3. Closely knit employee group				
4. Convenient location				
5. Desk job				
6. Different patients or clients each day				
7. Direct patient care				
8. Fast pace				
9. Flexible job description				
10. Flexible hours				
11. Job security				
12. Large organization				
13. Loosely knit employee group				
14. Low turnover among patients or clients				
15. Manual work with equipment, machines, etc.				
16. People contact, excluding hands-on care				
17. Physical activity				
18. Quiet surroundings				
19. Regular hours				
20. Short commute				
21. Small office				
22. Work with adults				
23. Work with children				

Introduction

Remember that you can practice a profession in one setting to achieve your short-term goals and move into a different setting as your career evolves.

Part 4: Job Satisfaction (What Keeps Me Going?)

You'll notice that items from this part of the self-assessment don't appear in the worker profiles in chapter 3. There are a couple of reasons. The satisfactions of *meaningful work* and *career advancement opportunities* are available in any health care job. Some advancement comes with promotions and pay raises, but often you need extra training.

Beyond that, each workplace is different. One nursing home may have a *supportive boss* (#8), the next one may not. Research is the only way to discover which work environments offer what you need.

Reward	4	3	2	1
1. Career advancement opportunities				
2. Congenial co-workers				
3. High salary				
4. Meaningful work				
5. Opportunity to apply specific skills				
6. Recognition for my contribution				
7. Specific job benefits (e.g., health insurance, tuition reimbursement, etc.)				
8. Supportive boss				

As you review your results, pick out the deal breakers—the "perks" or rewards you *must* have. They might be the 4-rated items for which you would sacrifice others. You might trade things like a high salary for attractive career advancement opportunities. If you take a child to school, or do not own a car, you might even accept less pay for a job close to home.

Introduction

Here's one last hint about job satisfaction and job setting choices: Choose your deal breakers carefully because there's a good chance you won't find everything you want in one job or one occupation. You'll be a lot happier if you leave a little space for compromise.

As you work your way through the rest of the book, glance back at your self-assessment often, so when you finish, you'll have a good foundation of self-knowledge on which to plan your next education and career choices.

WHERE CAN I LEARN MORE?

These resources offer more insights into skills and work preferences:

- *What Color Is Your Parachute? A Practical Manual for Job-Hunters & Career-Changers, 2002,* by Richard Nelson Bolles (Ten Speed Press, Berkeley, CA, 2001, $16.95). Updated annually, it's one of the best career-planning and self-assessment books. The job search and career-building techniques will serve you at any stage of your life.

- *Whistle While You Work: Heeding Your Life's Calling,* by Richard J. Leider and David A. Shapiro (Berrett-Koehler, San Francisco, CA, 2001, $15.95). Helps you identify work to match your gifts, aptitudes, passions and values. Shows how to find a job that suits you. The book features case studies and worksheets.

- www.careerexplorer.net features skill and aptitude inventories. The site also posts articles written by experts on discovering your skills and work preferences.

- www.UniversityOfLife.com links you to personality profiles and skills inventories. Some of the tests are fun, while others are serious.

Introduction

PERSONAL PROFILE

Alyson Guerrero
Registered Medical Assistant

Alyson always wanted to work in health care. "I like to work hands-on with people. At job fairs in high school, I was always fascinated by the medical exhibits," she says. As a high school student, she volunteered in a hospital. After graduation, she worked in an adult day care center with frail elderly clients. "I didn't have the grades or the money for a four-year college," she says. "The advantage of a technical training program is that you go for eight months and you're done."

That's exactly what Alyson did in 1983. She studied medical assisting. At that time, the registry exam was optional, but she took it anyway. "I'm in a career field where I know I could go anywhere and always have a job," she notes.

Today, Alyson is a "back office" medical assistant in an internal medicine practice. She takes X rays, draws blood, and prepares patients to see the doctor.

How Alyson Weaves Work With Her Personality and Family Life

As part of her training, Alyson worked in a minor emergency clinic. "It was exciting, but I never saw the same patients twice," she says. She finds that working in an internal medicine office suits her better. "It's more what I like—it's more structured. I know my patients; 95 percent of them are over 65 years old." She's worked there for 13 years and the patients regard her as their friend. "I'm very close to my patients," she says. "That's one of the reasons I prefer to work in a doctor's office instead of a hospital."

Another thing she likes about the doctor's office is the regular hours. Her evenings and weekends are reserved for family and for playing softball, which she and her husband enjoy as a couple.

While interactions with patients are generally smooth, Alyson notes that health care workers need strong personalities. "You have to be tolerant of people who are ill, because they can get ugly with you. You have be strong enough to let some things roll off your back."

How to Make the Most of Your Training and Externship

As one who's supervised medical assisting trainees, Alyson explains how to make a good impression: "Never sit there and do nothing. When you finish a task, ask others in the office what you can do for them. Offer to do their filing or stock their exam rooms. When you don't know something, don't be afraid to ask lots of questions. The medical field changes every day."

Trainees with that degree of initiative and interest in learning will be first to get the job offers. In fact, Alyson says, the offers will probably come before you complete your training.

Chapter One

AN OVERVIEW OF THE HEALTH CARE INDUSTRY

HEALTH CARE: THE BIG PICTURE

Are you looking for a career with job security and plenty of room to grow? Health care is all that and more. Of the 30 fastest-growing occupations in the country, 13 are in health care. "And wherever you work, there's always the inner satisfaction of knowing you're helping people," says Scott Bailey, chief financial officer at a cardiology clinic in San Antonio, Texas.

The health care industry employs more than 11 million people. There are opportunities to match almost any interest. For example, business offices in hospitals and clinics, medical research programs, and even medical libraries need nonclinical (support) employees. Hospitals and doctors' offices need a wide variety of clinical (direct patient care) employees. And you don't need years of schooling to get your foot in the door because most jobs require fewer than four years of training after high school.

If you seek opportunities for advancement, you'll find them. Many people use their first job as the first rung on the career ladder. "There are always new things to learn—this is a career, not a job," explains Ann Barker, R.N., B.S.N., who started as a hospital nurse and now heads up the medical assistant training at the Ohio Institute of Photography and Technology in Dayton. Since many of the jobs, especially in hospitals, need people around the clock, it's possible to go to school and earn an income at the same time.

Although it can be tricky to predict job growth in an industry, health care is a sure bet. You've heard of the Baby Boom generation? Those 76 million "boomers" born between 1946 and 1964 are now reaching their 50s, the age where people begin to need more health services. The boomers' parents are already in their 70s and 80s.

The aging of the boomers and their parents means that the elderly population will grow faster than any other age group in the next 10 years. When you add in the medical advances that save the lives of more sick and severely injured patients, you can see why health care jobs will grow faster than all other industries. The number of health care jobs will increase by 26 percent between now and 2008, compared to 15 percent for other industries.

Along with a huge demand for medical care will be an equal demand for dental services. Thanks to new discoveries in tooth and gum care, most people can keep their natural teeth throughout their lives instead of replacing them with dentures or false teeth as in the past. This means dental offices will need trained staff.

Health care organizations come in all forms and sizes, from large inner-city hospitals employing thousands, to small-town doctors with only one medical assistant. In fact, over half of all health service organizations (not counting hospitals) employ fewer than five workers. On the other end of the spectrum, two out of three hospitals employ more than 1,000 workers, from pharmacy assistants to audiovisual technicians to medical supply clerks.

A Guided Tour of the World of Health Care

Health care takes place in just about any setting you can imagine: small offices where the staff is like a family and they know their patients well, bustling hospitals where phones ring constantly and people make life and death decisions, neighborhood clinics where you might hear conversations in Spanish as well as Vietnamese and English.

If you're like a lot of folks, you may think doctors and nurses have a corner on the best health care jobs. "When I was young," Scott Bailey recalls, "I'd drive by a hospital and think of all the doctors and nurses working there. What I didn't realize, until I got into health care, is that other workers outnumber them by far and that most of those other jobs don't take a four-year college degree or more."

An Overview of the Health Care Industry

> **WHERE DO THEY WORK?**
>
> As you might guess, hospitals write the paychecks for most health care workers. Here's a breakdown of how the health care workforce is divided. The U.S. Bureau of Labor Statistics predicts that this picture will be the same for the next five to seven years.
>
> | | |
> |---|---|
> | Hospitals | 40 percent |
> | Medical offices | 18 percent |
> | Nursing and personal care facilities | 18 percent |
> | Home health care services | 7 percent |
> | Dental offices | 6 percent |
> | Other health practitioners | 4 percent |
> | Allied health services | 3 percent |
> | Medical and dental laboratories | 2 percent |
>
> (Numbers do not add up to 100 percent due to rounding.)
>
> Source: U.S. Department of Labor, 2000–01 Occupational Outlook Handbook

Let's take a closer look at the health industry. Along the way, you'll see the job outlook for each segment.

Hospitals

Job growth through 2008: 8 percent

Hospitals provide a wide scope of services from diagnostic (finding the cause of an illness) to surgery, emergency treatment, and care for the sick. Some take care of the general run of health problems. Others specialize in care for cancer patients (oncology), children (pediatrics), or the mentally ill (psychiatric), for example.

While hospital stays of a week or more used to be common, that's all changing. Care is shifting to outpatient settings—doctor's offices, same-day surgery and clinics, for example. So you'll find that many hospitals have branched out into home health care services and rehab units.

Hospitals employ the widest variety of workers. Twenty-five percent are registered nurses. Other workers include nursing aides, food service, and janitorial people. Also on board are respiratory therapy technicians, office staff, arts and craft workers, and building maintenance specialists.

Personal Care Facilities

Job growth through 2008: 26 percent

Nursing and personal care facilities serve people who need less skilled medical care than hospitals provide. These facilities are staffed mainly by nursing aides. Most of the patients are elderly. However, some places specialize in rehabilitation for people who suffer sports injuries, auto accidents, strokes, burns, heart attacks, or other problems.

Assisted living is part of this category. This type of care allows people to live independently while providing the help they need. Most of the residents are frail elderly who need help bathing or feeding themselves or remembering their medications. Others suffer from incontinence, confusion, or even Alzheimer's disease. Assisted living facilities can include private homes that take care of a few people, but more often they're apartment complexes for several hundred.

Medical Offices and Clinics

Job growth through 2008: 41 percent

Doctors usually practice in groups or clinics. Sometimes each physician in the group will have a different type practice or specialty, such as primary care (also known as family practice), diabetes, or cardiology (heart problems). In other settings, each physician has the same specialty. Forty percent of the staff in medical offices and clinics are medical receptionists and secretaries.

Home Health Care Services

Job growth through 2008: 80 percent

Most of the patients here are elderly. They might receive services such as breathing treatments or physical therapy to help them rebuild strength after a stroke or heart attack. Often, however, home care consists of help with bathing, meal preparation, or laundry. The demand for home care will increase right along with the rising numbers of senior citizens because most people would rather stay in their own homes as long as possible. Besides, home care costs less than a nursing home, except for those who need care around the clock.

Fifty percent of the personnel are personal care and home health aides. Also on staff are nurses and nursing aides, as well as physical, occupational, and speech therapists and aides.

Dental Offices and Clinics

Job growth through 2008: 30 percent

These are usually small offices employing a few workers. Some do general dentistry while others specialize. Among dental specialties you'll find surgery, periodontal (gum) care and orthodontics (braces).

In dental offices and clinics, 33 percent of workers are dental assistants. You'll also find dental hygienists. Larger offices employ dental laboratory technicians, office managers, and administrative staff.

Other Health Practitioners

Job growth through 2008: 43 percent

Here we find chiropractors (adjustments of the spine and joints), optometrists (measurement and fitting of eye glasses and contact lenses), and podiatrists (foot care). There are also physical and occupational therapists, psychologists, audiologists (hearing specialists), speech-language therapists, and dietitians. As public demand grows for what are known as complementary therapies, we'll see more professionals offering acupuncture (treatment of ailments like back pain by inserting fine needles into the skin at strategic points), hypnosis, and massage therapy. Forty percent of the workers in these settings are in administrative roles.

Allied Health Services

Job growth through 2008: 65 percent

These establishments provide services like kidney dialysis, drug treatment, and rehabilitation; they also run blood banks and teach childbirth preparation classes. Allied health services hire social and human service assistants to work with the social workers, registered nurses, and psychologists.

Medical and Dental Laboratories

Job growth through 2008: 24 percent

In medical labs, workers analyze the blood and urine samples from the hospitals and doctors' offices. In dental labs, they make dentures (false teeth), artificial teeth for implants and orthodontic appliances. The majority of workers here are laboratory and radiologic (x-ray) technologists or technicians.

> **DID YOU KNOW?**
>
> Health care is a great place to find a part-time job. Students and parents of young children make up much of the workforce.
>
> Since many services stay open around the clock (24/7) there are opportunities for shift work and flexible hours.
>
> - 36 percent of workers in dental offices are part time.
> - 20 percent of workers in medical offices are part time.
> - Home health care is one of the fastest-growing segments of the U.S. economy.
> - Every state needs health care workers, but the greatest needs are in California, New York, Florida, Texas, and Pennsylvania.
> - Some facilities train workers for entry-level positions, but if you have had some formal training when you apply, you will have an edge for both patient care and administrative jobs.

Occupational Hazards

As in any line of work, health care jobs have some hazards. In direct patient care, back strain can occur from lifting patients and equipment. Also, there's the danger of exposure to radiation and caustic chemicals. Once in a great while, care givers contract infectious disease such as AIDS, tuberculosis, or hepatitis. However, health care workers are trained in safety measures that can eliminate all but the rare injury.

Of course, it's one thing to learn safe practices and another to use them without exception. "You just cannot be careless!" warns Alyson Guerrero. "My patients ask me all the time if I get tired of wearing the mask and gloves when I draw blood. But I would no more think of drawing blood without a mask and gloves than I would think of driving a car without a seatbelt."

Money Matters

Your earnings in health care will depend on your level of training and responsibility. Larger hospitals and medical practices often pay a little more and salaries vary depending on where you choose to live. In general, you can expect to see these average hourly wages:

An Overview of the Health Care Industry

AVERAGE HOURLY WAGES

Registered nurses	$19
Licensed practical nurses	$13
Dental assistants	$11
Medical assistants	$10.25
Receptionists and information clerks	$10
General office clerks	$9.50
Home health aides	$8.50
Nursing aides, orderlies, and attendants	$8
Maids and housekeeping staff	$7.50

Source, U.S. Bureau of Labor Statistics

Some employers, especially hospitals, are intent on keeping good staff, so they offer tuition reimbursement or pay for training. Most hospitals pay extra for weekend shifts, holidays, or late shifts.

But, no matter how attractive the earnings or the working conditions, it will get old in a hurry if you go into health care with false impressions. Although the people you'll meet in the pages of this book love the work, they caution that the hours can be long and some patients are rude or uncooperative. "It can get tough if you're in it just for the money. You'll begin to hate the work. You need to love people and have a basic interest in the field so that when those things happen, you'll know you're doing something you like," advises Roland Cutting, dental manager at a children's dental center in San Antonio, Texas.

WHERE CAN I LEARN MORE?

The U.S. Bureau of Labor maintains a huge website of useful information. For example, the *Occupational Outlook Handbook* features descriptions of health care jobs. The search engine makes it easy to navigate. Go to www.bls.gov.

For general career planning as well as articles on specific health care occupations, check out www.careerplanning.about.com.

An Overview of the Health Care Industry

PERSONAL PROFILE

Loyda Morales
Registered Medical Assistant

Loyda, 29, works in a family practice office with one physician and another medical assistant. She handles the back office—blood draws, blood pressures, EKGs, and the like—while her co-worker takes care of the desk. Since the practice takes only walk-in appointments, Loyda never knows what the day will hold, but she does know it'll be busy.

Looking back, Loyda says, "Going on to school is the best decision I ever made." She enrolled at the San Antonio College of Medical and Dental Assistants (SACMDA) in San Antonio, Texas after seven years at McDonald's, as well as jobs in home improvement stores, toy stores, and a day care center.

What Loyda Loves about Her Work
It's the learning, she says without a moment's hesitation. "I have a boss who loves to teach and every day there's something new to learn. And I love my patients."

Loyda's Biggest Challenge and How She Copes With It
It boils down to insurance. "I don't understand how insurance companies can turn people down when they need care," she contends. Her boss helps by doing as much as possible for each patient and encouraging Loyda and her co-worker to follow suit.

Where Loyda Plans to Go From Here
Currently, she's taking night classes toward a bachelor's degree in nursing and a master's degree in biology. Loyda's long-range goal is to go to medical school.

Most Valuable Part of the Medical Aassisting Studies
"I enjoyed the learning experience the most," she recalls. "And I had a good time connecting with my teachers and classmates." Loyda has kept in touch with some of her teachers since graduation in 1998.

Looking back on her studies, she notes that "everything we learned makes sense when you're in the field. It all connects."

What Loyda Wishes She Had Known Earlier
"I wish I'd started earlier!" she says. Not realizing what educational options were available, Loyda went to work right out of high school. "I wish there'd been more information about schools like SACMDA when I graduated.

"This kind of program is good for the person who wants a degree but doesn't have the time or money to stay in college for three or four years." Within 11 or 12 months, she explains, you can get a job and then go for more education.

A Tip for the Uncertain
"Volunteer at a hospital or a nursing home, or even work at the Special Olympics (for the developmentally disabled) to see if you're cut out for health care. If you find you have any interest, don't wait to go to school," Loyda says.

Chapter Two

WORKING IN HEALTH CARE

FINDING THE JOB THAT'S RIGHT FOR YOU

Now that you know about the unlimited career opportunities in health care, you're probably thinking, "OK, where do I start?" It'll be easy to spot jobs that might suit you after reviewing your results from the self-assessment tools in the Introduction. Keep them in mind like a "yardstick." With each description, ask yourself:

1. What kind of work picture is this?
2. Would I fit into this picture?
3. Would I like to be in this picture?

"Health care offers something to fit any interest," explains Debbie Schroller, director of Career Services at the San Antonio College of Medical and Dental Assistants in San Antonio, Texas. "There are 'front office' responsibilities like coding medical procedures, handling the information technology duties, transcribing medical reports, and billing. The 'back office' people do hands-on patient care like taking blood pressures, drawing blood or preparing patients for their exams." Health care isn't going away, she adds. "There will always be sick people who need good care givers and the computers that run the system are definitely here to stay," she adds.

As an insider, Debbie cautions that the media sometimes glorify health care. Much of healing and helping people live with health problems is quiet work. It takes place behind the scenes, she says. "We need qualified people in nursing homes, and people to work with children and cancer patients."

Working in Health Care

"We need lab technicians to seek cures for diseases. We need orthopaedic technicians to build prosthetics for adults and children. We need nurses aides to back up the registered nurses in hospital wards. We need pharmacy technicians to get the right medication to the right patient on time. Last, but certainly not least, we need people who are good with numbers or paperwork. After all, people get very upset when they have mistakes on their bills."

Every medical and dental office needs people with warm smiles to comfort patients when they're sick or in pain. And if you've ever had blood drawn, you know how important it is to have an expert phlebotomist who can stick your arm without hurting you!

EVALUATING YOUR CAREER OPTIONS

If you know exactly which health care job you want, you could skip to chapter 4, "Preparing for Your Career." But you might miss something if you do. The profiles of health care "hot jobs" in this chapter could open your eyes to choices you hadn't considered.

If you're like most people who think they'd like to work in health care, you're not sure how to narrow down the choices. That's not surprising, notes Carol Ellstrom, B.S.N., R.N., manager of Education and Staff Development at Paradise Valley Hospital in National City, California. "The possibilities are endless, and the nicest part is that most of the positions can be used as stepping stones in your career," she explains.

One of the best ways to find your niche is through informal research:
- Volunteer several hours a week in a hospital, clinic, nursing home, or assisted living facility. Arrange this through the organization's volunteer office or human resources department.
- "Shadow" a health care professional. In other words, accompany the person through his normal work routine for a couple days. Set this up through your high school counselor or the organization's representative at a job fair. Or use the channels for volunteering, described above.
- Discuss your interests and goals with the admissions counselor at a college or vocational school.

Working in Health Care

> **TERMS OF THE TRADE**
>
> As you read through the book, certain words will pop up repeatedly. Here are definitions as they apply to health care:
>
> **Clinical:** Direct patient care.
>
> **Externship:** Period of occupational training in which a student works, under close supervision, in a real job setting. Externships are also called *field placements*, *field experience*, or *field training*.
>
> **Nonclinical:** Does not involve direct patient care.
>
> **Inpatient:** Type of care, usually in a hospital, where patients spend 24 hours or more.
>
> **Outpatient:** Type of care, usually in a clinic or physician's office, where patients arrive and leave in less than 24 hours. Outpatient care is also called ambulatory care.
>
> **Technician:** Worker whose job requires entry-level skills. For example, a technician prepares blood for a lab test and performs the test.
>
> **Technologist:** Worker whose job requires higher-level skills and experience. For example, a technologist does a preliminary interpretation of a lab test and might confer with the doctor about the patient's diagnosis based on the test results.

HOT JOBS IN HEALTH CARE

Though we can't begin to list *all* the occupations in health care, we can introduce you to those with high growth and relatively short training requirements. The U.S. Bureau of Labor Statistics (BLS) reports that almost half of our country's 30 fastest growing occupations—"hot jobs"—are in health care. Qualifications include on-the-job training, certificates, bachelor's degrees, or master's degrees.

In the list below, you'll find seven of the 13 health care jobs from the "hot list." Some require lengthy training—four to five years. Professionals in those positions usually supervise workers in related, less skilled occupations. Look for the remaining six hot jobs in chapter 3, "Career Close-Ups." They represent many job openings and require fewer than two years of training.

Occupational therapists, for example, evaluate patients and design care plans. They delegate the routine tasks of implementation to occupational therapy assistants and aids. Other jobs described in this chapter are transitional—short stops on the career ladder where people work while training for the next step. Other occupations described here offer relatively few openings despite the high growth. The job descriptions are based on material from the 2000–01 *Occupational Outlook Handbook*, published by the U.S. Bureau of Labor Statistics.

The rest of this chapter introduces you to the range of options available in health care—everything from providing bedside care to using sophisticated testing equipment. Besides the exciting variety of work, health care accounts for 13 of the thirty jobs on the Department of Labor's list of fastest growing occupations.

1. Ambulance Drivers and Attendants

(not including emergency medical technicians—EMTs)
Job openings by 2008: 26,000
Growth from 1998–2008: 35 percent

Points of Interest:
- Ambulance driving is exciting and stressful work.
- Drivers sometimes hold these jobs while training for higher-level health care positions.
- Companies often require recruits to have basic EMT certification.

What Do Ambulance Drivers and Attendants Do?

Drivers take the wheel of the vehicle while attendants navigate, help lift patients, and administer first aid. The work often takes place amid life and death circumstances—auto accidents, heart attacks, drownings, childbirth, gunshot wounds, or sports accidents.

Ambulance drivers and attendants must have the ability to remain calm and clearheaded, and to follow instructions from other emergency personnel in the midst of chaos. Drivers must handle their vehicles safely in all kinds of weather and road conditions, day and night. Both drivers and attendants must be able to find their way in unfamiliar locations. The jobs demand patience during periods of down time and the capacity to snap into crisis mode at a moment's notice. The hours can be long and irregular.

What is the Ambulance Driver's and Attendant's Training?

Some companies require a Red Cross first-aid training certificate. Drivers and attendants learn to operate ambulances and to coordinate their work with EMTs through on-the-job training.

How Much Do Ambulance Drivers and Attendants Earn?

Salaries range from $8.00 to $11.00 an hour.

Where Can I Learn More?

- Call local ambulance companies listed in the Yellow Pages under *ambulance service*.
- One of the largest medical transportation services, American Medical Response, operates ambulance services nationwide.

    American Medical Response
    Phone: (303) 615-8500; toll-free job line (877) 267-5627
    Website: www.amr-inc.com

2. Registered Nurses with a Bachelor of Science (B.S.N.) degree

Job openings by 2008: 2,530,000 (For all registered nurses, including those with a B.S.N.)
Growth from 1998–2008: 30 percent

Points of Interest:

- Most administrative positions require at least a B.S.N.
- Due to high demand, B.S.N. nurses can often choose from several job offers.
- B.S.N. nurses have more advancement opportunities than do associate's degree or diploma nurses.

What Are a B.S.N. Nurse's Responsibilities?

Nurses with B.S.N. training advance in either clinical care or administrative directions. The clinical responsibilities involve such specializations as nurse practitioners, certified nurse-midwives, or certified registered nurse anesthetists. In the administrative or business areas, nurses oversee the nursing department in hospitals, work in quality assurance, or marketing.

Where Do B.S.N. Nurses Work?
- Hospitals (60 percent)
- Physicians' offices
- Nursing homes
- Home health agencies
- County and state public health departments
- Private business and industry

What is the B.S.N. Training?

Approximately 550 nursing programs, most located in colleges and universities, offer B.S.N. degrees. The training takes four to five years. Course work covers anatomy, physiology, microbiology, chemistry, nutrition, psychology, and nursing techniques. To round out their education, students take electives in liberal arts subjects. They have supervised clinical training in hospital departments including pediatrics, psychiatry, maternity and surgery. Many programs also provide experience in nursing homes, public health department, home health agencies and outpatient clinics.

The familiar "R.N." credential signifies that the nurse holds a registered nurse license required by every state. To qualify, candidates must graduate from an accredited nursing program and pass a national licensing exam.

How Much Do B.S.N. Nurses Earn?

Salaries range from $40,000 to $50,000 a year. Physicians' offices and nursing homes pay at the lower end of the range.

Where Can I Learn More?
- For career and training information, contact:
  National League for Nursing
  Phone: (800) 669-1665
  Website: www.nln.org

- For the names of B.S.N. programs, contact:

  American Association of Colleges of Nursing
  Phone: (202) 463-6930
  Website:www.aacn.nche.edu

- For general nursing information, contact:

  American Nurses Association
  Phone: (202) 651-7000
  Website: www.nursingworld.org

3. Cardiovascular Technologists and Technicians

Job openings by 2008: 29,000
Growth from 1998–2008: 39 percent

Points of Interest:

- In spite of the fast growth, the number of job openings for cardiovascular technologists and technicians will remain low because the occupational field itself is relatively small.
- Most employers fill positions by training people already in the health care field.
- Cardiovascular technologists and technicians generally work 40-hour weeks that may include weekends, some evenings, and on-call shifts.
- The work involves a lot of walking and standing.
- Jobs in heart catheterization labs involve contact with seriously ill patients who may suffer life threatening complications during their procedures.

What Do Cardiovascular Technologists and Technicians Do?

The simple answer is that they help doctors diagnose and treat heart (cardiac) and blood vessel (peripheral vascular) ailments. Besides working with patients, these professionals operate highly sophisticated equipment. Some handle administrative functions such as scheduling appointments or maintaining patient records. Apart from the general responsibilities, there are distinct specialties within the field.

1. Cardiology technologists assist physicians with "invasive" heart procedures: They insert a small tube or catheter through a blood vessel in the patient's leg and into the heart. In balloon angioplasty, the catheter carries a tiny, inflated bag that opens a blocked blood vessel in the heart. The technologist monitors the electrocardiogram (EKG) equipment and notifies the physician if problems arise. Some cardiology technologists monitor patients during open heart surgery and assist in implanting pacemakers.

2. Vascular technologists use ultrasound instruments to record blood pressure, blood oxygen levels and blood circulation in the brain. For these "noninvasive" tests, electrodes or special patches are placed on the patient's body. The electrodes are wired to ultrasound instruments that report the sound waves in the form of line patterns on a computer screen.

3. Echocardiographers use ultrasound equipment to collect and transmit sound waves from the heart.

4. Electrocardiograph (EKG or ECG) technicians take electrocardiograms or EKGs. This test traces electrical impulses transmitted by electrodes placed on the patient's chest, arms and legs. EKGs are done routinely prior to surgery on patients of all ages, and in physical exams for older people.

EKG technicians with advanced training conduct other noninvasive procedures, specifically Holter monitoring and stress testing. For Holter monitoring, they place electrodes on the patient's chest and attach a portable EKG monitor to the patient's belt. The patient wears the device for one or two days, and then returns it to the technician. The technician then prints the information for the physician, who uses it to diagnose heart problems. For stress tests, the technician connects the patient to an EKG monitor and records the heart rate while the patient walks on a treadmill.

In the next few years, EKG technicians trained in Holter monitoring and stress testing will have better job prospects than those who can perform only basic EKGs. This is because hospitals are training nursing aides and other workers in basic EKG procedures.

Where Do Cardiovascular Technologists and Technicians Work?
- Hospitals, in both inpatient units and outpatient clinics (80 percent)
- Cardiologists' offices (physicians specializing in heart problems), cardiac rehabilitation centers and ambulatory (same day) surgery centers (20 percent)

Working in Health Care

What Is a Cardiovascular Technologists' and Technicians' Training?

Although some cardiovascular technologists, vascular technologists, and echocardiographers receive on-the-job training, it's on the way out. The trend is toward two- to four-year training programs.

Cardiology technologists generally complete a two-year junior or community college program with one year of core courses and a year of specialized instruction. Students with previous health training and experience need only the year of specialized instruction. Graduates from programs accredited by the Joint Review Committee on Education in Cardiovascular Technology may register as professional technologists with the American Registry of Diagnostic Medical Sonographers or Cardiovascular Credentialing International. (See "Where can I learn more?" below.)

There are one-year certificate programs for basic EKGs, Holter monitoring and stress testing, however, most EKG technicians are trained on the job by an EKG supervisor or cardiologist. That training usually lasts eight to 16 weeks. For on-the-job training, employers usually choose people who already have health knowledge and experience, such as nursing aides.

How Much Do Cardiovascular Technologists and Technicians Earn?

For cardiology technologists, salaries range widely from $23,000 to $49,000. For EKG technicians, the range is $16,000 to $39,000.

Where Can I Learn More?

- For general information about careers in cardiovascular technology, contact:
  Alliance of Cardiovascular Professionals
  Phone: (757) 497-1225
  Website: www.acp-online.org

- For a list of accredited programs in cardiovascular technology, contact:
  Joint Review Committee on Education in Cardiovascular Technology
  Phone: (410) 418-4800

- For information on vascular technology, contact:
  Society of Vascular Technology
  Phone: (301) 459-7550
  Website: www.svtnet.org

- To learn more about echocardiography, contact:
  American Society of Echocardiography
  Phone: (919) 787-5181
  Website: www.asecho.org

- For information on registration and certification, contact:
  Cardiovascular Credentialing International
  Phone: (800) 326-0268
  Website: www.cci-online.org

  American Registry of Diagnostic Medical Sonographers
  Phone: (800) 541-9754
  Website: ardms.org

4. Dental Hygienists

Job openings by 2008: 201,000
Growth from 1998–2008: 41 percent

Points of Interest:
- The demand for dental hygienists will be driven by population growth and improved dental practices enabling people to keep their natural teeth throughout their lives.
- Opportunities for part-time work and flexible hours are common in this field. Hygienists often have their choice of evening or weekend hours, as well two- or three-day weeks.
- Many professionals earn full-time salaries by holding part-time jobs in dental offices.
- About 60 percent of dental hygienists work fewer than 35 hours a week.
- Hygienists must protect themselves from infectious diseases by wearing safety glasses, surgical masks, and gloves.

What Do Dental Hygienists Do?

Hygienists clean teeth and teach patients tooth and gum care. In fact, patient education is a major part of the job. They also shoot and develop dental X rays. In some states, they're licensed to administer oral anesthetics and anesthetic gas, and to prepare and place temporary fillings. Some states even allow hygienists to remove sutures after oral surgery.

Where Do Dental Hygienists Work?
- Private dental offices
- Public school systems
- Public health agencies
- Federal and state government agencies

What Is a Dental Hygienist's Training?
Most dental hygienists earn an associate's degree. About half of the training programs prefer applicants who have completed one year of college. Currently, about 250 schools offer accredited programs. Basic training includes courses in anatomy, physiology, chemistry, microbiology, pharmacology, nutrition, radiography, periodontology (study of gum diseases, dental materials, dental hygiene and behavioral sciences). A bachelor's or master's degree in dental hygiene is usually required for research, teaching or practice in public health agencies or school health programs.

Hygienists must be licensed by the state in which they practice. All states use the exam administered by the American Dental Association Joint Commission on National Dental Examinations.

How Much Do Dental Hygienists Earn?
Hourly wages range from $17.00 to $38.00, depending on geographic location, employment setting and years of experience. Private dental offices pay by the hour, day, year, or on a commission basis. Dental hygienists in school systems, public health agencies, state or federal agencies are likely to earn attractive salaries and substantial benefits.

Where Can I Learn More?
- For career information and educational requirements, contact:
    Division of Professional Development
    American Dental Hygienists Association
    Phone: (312) 440-8900
    Website: www.adha.org

Working in Health Care

- For a list of accredited programs and educational requirements, contact:
  Commission on Dental Accreditation
  Website: www.ada.org/prof/ed/index.asp

- To learn more about state licensing requirements, call the local State Board of Dental Examiners. Find the listing in the White Pages state government section or call your public library.

5. Occupational Therapists (OTs)

Job openings by 2008: 98,000
Growth from 1998–2008: 34 percent

Points of Interest:

- Demand for occupational therapy will rise as baby boomers age and confront problems like strokes, heart attacks and arthritis that require rehabilitation and modified living arrangements.
- School districts will need more OTs as more children with disabilities enter special education programs.
- More than 25 percent of OTs work part time.
- About 10 percent of OTs hold more than one job.
- The trend is toward OTs taking supervisory positions while overseeing the work of OT aides and assistants.

What Do OTs Do?

OTs help people improve their ability to perform the tasks of their personal and work lives. Their clients have disabilities stemming from mental, physical, developmental, or emotional problems. The services help people improve their basic physical skills, such as preparing meals or using a computer with a partially paralyzed hand. They also help people compensate for permanent loss of function, such as blindness or memory loss, in which case they might teach clients how to do basic tasks.

In cases of permanent disability such as spinal cord injuries, cerebral palsy, or muscular dystrophy, OTs instruct clients in the use of adaptive equipment—wheelchairs, splints, and aids for eating and dressing. They also design or make adaptive equipment for home and workplace.

Some OTs work in industrial settings. Others specialize in certain age groups or disabilities. Specialties also include elementary and secondary schools, mental illness, substance abuse and emotional disorders.

Where Do OTs Work?
- Hospitals: General, rehabilitation, and psychiatric (more than 50 percent)
- School systems
- Occupational therapy offices and clinics
- Home health agencies
- Nursing homes
- Community mental health centers
- Adult daycare programs
- Job training services
- Residential care facilities for the developmentally disabled
- Private practices

What Is an OT's Training?

The minimum requirement for practice is a four-year bachelor's degree in OT. For licensure, all states require graduation from an accredited school and successful completion of a national certification exam resulting in the title "registered occupational therapist." There are 88 bachelor's degree programs in the United States, 11 post-bachelor's certificate programs for students with a bachelor's degree in another field, and 53 master's degree programs. While most schools offer full-time programs, a growing number offer weekend or part-time alternatives.

Outside of the core courses in physical, biological and behavioral sciences, and basic OT skills, training includes six months of field work.

How Much Do OTs Earn?

Most salaries range from $31,000 to $86,000. OTs in nursing homes and personal care facilities command the highest pay, those in school systems command the least.

Working in Health Care

Where Can I Learn More?
- For career information and a list of accredited programs, contact:
American Occupational Therapy Association
Phone: (301) 652-2682
Website: www.adha.org

6. Physician Assistants (PAs)

Job openings by 2008: 98,000
Growth from 1998–2008: 58 percent

Points of Interest:
- The number of jobs is greater than the number of PAs.
- PAs who work in doctors' offices often make early morning hospital rounds and may be on call some weekends and nights.
- Employment opportunities are especially hot in areas with few physicians, such as inner cities and rural communities.

What Are a PA's Responsibilities?

PAs perform a wide range of complex services under the supervision of a physician. You might say that a PA is like a second pair of hands for the physician. In general, the duties are determined by the supervising physician and the laws of the state in which the PA practices. PAs take medical histories, examine patients, or order and interpret laboratory tests. They evaluate and diagnose symptoms, such as sore throats or knee pain. In most states, they are licensed to prescribe medications. PAs also suture cuts, perform minor surgery and put splints and casts on injured limbs.

Some PAs work in rural or inner city clinics where the physician comes in one or two days a week. All PAs make regular reports to their supervisors and contact them immediately if confronted with a case that's beyond their expertise.

Where Do PAs Work?
- Medical offices and clinics, including primary care, pediatrics, orthopaedics, radiology, and public health clinics
- Inpatient and outpatient surgery
- Hospital emergency rooms
- Nursing homes
- Home health agencies
- Prisons

What Is a PA's Training?
Most PAs have a bachelor's degree. Others have a certificate, associate degree or a master's degree. There are approximately 116 accredited PA training programs. Admission requirements vary, though many require two years of college and some work experience in health care. Programs generally last two years. They're based in four-year colleges, schools of allied health, community colleges, university medical centers, or hospitals.

PA students take course work in the basic medical sciences including biochemistry, nutrition, human anatomy, physiology, clinical pharmacology, and disease prevention. They do several "rotations" (externships) under the supervision of physicians, which might include psychiatry, pediatrics, or obstetrics and gynecology (pregnancy, childbirth, and women's health).

All states and the District of Columbia require that PAs graduate from an accredited training program and pass the Physician Assistants National Certifying Examination, administered by the National Commission on Certification of Physician Assistants (NCCPA).

How Much Do PAs Earn?
Salaries range from $25,000 to $71,500; most earn about $47,000. Incomes vary according to specialty, practice setting, geographic location and years of experience.

Working in Health Care

Where Can I Learn More?
- For career information, contact:

    American Academy of Physician Assistants
    Phone: (703) 836-2272
    Website: www.aapa.org

- For a list of accredited programs, contact:

    Association of Physician Assistant Programs
    Phone: (703) 548-5538
    Website: www.apap.org

7. Surgical Technologists

Job openings by 2008: 77,000
Growth from 1998–2008: 42 percent

Points of Interest:
- The demand for surgical technologists will increase as the number of surgical procedures grows.
- A few surgical technologists, known as "private scrubs," are employed directly by surgeons who assemble special surgical teams, such as those for liver transplants.
- Although hospitals will continue to employ most of the surgical technologists, faster rates of job growth will be in doctors' offices and clinics, including outpatient or ambulatory surgical centers.
- Some surgical technologists manage central supply departments in hospitals, or work with insurance companies, sterile supply services, and surgical equipment firms.

What Do Surgical Technologists Do?

Surgical technologists (also called *surgical* or *operating room technicians*) assist in operations under the supervision of surgeons, registered nurses or other professionals. They prepare surgical instruments and check equipment. They check patients' vital signs, and shave and sterilize incision sites. They also help the surgical team scrub and put on their gowns, gloves and masks. During surgery, they operate some of the equipment, pass instruments, maintain the blood supplies for transfusions and assist with dressings. After surgery, they transfer patients to the recovery room and prepare the operating room for the next case.

Experienced surgical technologists may advance by specializing in a certain type of surgery, such as open heart or neurosurgery (procedures on the brain or spine). With additional training, some surgical technologists become first assistants with duties including suturing, cauterizing blood vessels, closing or treating wounds.

Where Do Surgical Technologists Work?
- Hospitals (more than 60 percent)
- Clinics and surgical centers
- Offices of doctors and dentists who perform outpatient surgery
- Special surgical teams headed by one surgeon

What Is a Surgical Technologist's Training?
Training lasts from nine to 24 months. Graduates earn a certificate, diploma or associate degree. Shorter programs are available for licensed practical nurses or military personnel with the appropriate training. Voluntary certification as a certified surgical technologist (CST) is available to graduates of accredited programs who pass a national exam. There are 165 accredited programs in the United States.

Course work includes anatomy, physiology, microbiology, pharmacology, professional ethics, and medical terminology. Students learn how to drape and transfer patients as well as sterilization of instruments, infection control and equipment maintenance. Training also includes supervised clinical experience.

How Much Do Surgical Technologists Earn?
Salaries range from $19,000 to $36,000.

Where Can I Learn More?
- For career information and a list of CAAHEP-accredited programs, contact:
  Association of Surgical Technologists
  Phone: (303) 694-9130
  Website: www.ast.org

- To learn about certification requirements, contact:

  Liaison Council on Certification for the Surgical Technologist
  Phone: (303) 694-9264
  Website: www.lcc-st.org/index_ie.htm

WHAT EMPLOYERS LOOK FOR IN APPLICANTS

Now that you've had a peek at a few health care jobs, take a moment to listen to a bit of advice from some managers who do the hiring. For openers, they all say, "When you apply for a job, bring your attitude!" While a positive attitude isn't the whole story, those who don't have one need not apply. It's that simple.

"First and foremost, I look for enthusiasm," says Carol Ellstrom, who's been teaching, hiring, and recommending health care professionals for over 20 years. If an applicant shows that key quality, she then looks at the school record: elective courses, internships or externships, three-and five-year career goals. "Those things help us pinpoint your interests," she explains. While grade-point average is important, it's not the whole story, Ellstrom adds. The letters of recommendation speak volumes. "In spite of constraints on the language instructors are allowed to use in their letters, an employer can tell which letters are routine and which are written for the student who really stands out. We sift the stand-out letters from the routine letters," she says.

Here's another piece of advice from Ellstrom: "Research your training program well. Know that it's what you really want to do. Once you find it, go into it heart and soul. When you get into the field, be enthusiastic about your work. We need people who are good and who bring others into their professions."

> **WORD TO THE WISE**
>
> From Scott Bailey, chief financial officer, Cardiology Clinic of San Antonio: "The heart of your job comes to this: how well you work with others. Remember that people are people, no matter where you are."

Jennifer Jacoby, R.N., M.S.N., chief nursing officer at Sharp Health Care in San Diego, California, likes applicants who research the jobs for which they apply. "What's even better," she says, "is to have that applicant explain how her skills are right for the job."

Ellstrom notes that while all health care professionals need compassion and people skills, there are niches for those who would rather work behind the scenes where there is less patient interaction. In hospital service departments, for instance, people order, inventory and distribute supplies and equipment. Pharmacy technicians stock medications and fill drug orders. "Surgical technology is another profession that involves little patient contact because your patients are asleep," Ellstrom says. "But of course, you have to get along with your coworkers."

Jacoby places a high priority on dependability. "People are counting on you," she says. "Naturally, you shouldn't come in when you are sick, but if you know that your schedule is going to change, tell your supervisor as far in advance as possible," she urges. "And when you say you'll do something, do it!"

An Employer's Wish List

If you can show an employer the following traits, you'll be a prime candidate for health care jobs, according to Jennifer Jacoby, Roland Cutting, and Scott Bailey.

- An even temperament and slow to anger. Health care jobs sometimes require long hours. "You'll be dealing with stressful situations and people can be difficult because they're sick, in pain, frightened, or frustrated," Cutting says. "You have to be motivated, and you have to be able to remember why you're there."
- A "can-do" attitude. "An employee who wants to do the minimum just to get by won't last long," Cutting says. "If somebody needs a volunteer, be the first in line."
- Curiosity. "I look for a person who's hungry to learn and isn't afraid to ask questions," Cutting says.
- Verbal and written communication skills. That includes a friendly voice, clear enunciation of health care terms, courteous telephone manner, good eye contact, accurate typing, and legible handwriting.
- More interest in the work than in the pay. "If an applicant asks first about the pay, that's a red flag," Cutting says. "I look for somebody who asks about the job first."

> **WORD TO THE WISE**
>
> From Kristin Gargano, B.S., R.R.P., department head for Medical Assisting at the Nebraska College of Business:
>
> "Certificate programs are a great way to break into health care. Within just a few months, you'll be qualified for a job. Then you can look around at what's out there. If something interests you, that's the time to think about a two- or four-year college program."
>
> "One of the best tracks today is Medical Assistant. With this credential, you can go wherever you want. These are multiskilled professionals—they draw blood, take X rays, and do injections—or, they can do administrative work in the 'front office,' billing and coding of medical records." As a stepping stone, this program is ideal, she adds. "Within 15 months, you can earn a diploma; in just 18 months, you can earn your associate's degree."

Portrait of a Star Employee

This is the employee supervisors recommend for promotions, awards and pay raises:

- Comes to work on time every day.
- Attends employer-sponsored workshops, even when they're not required.
- Asks questions.
- Shows initiative.
- Helps others if he finishes his work early.
- Checks her work for accuracy and completeness.
- Masters each aspect of his job, even if it takes extra study on his own time.
- Understands that "customer service" begins with her coworkers and extends to people outside of her immediate area. For instance, when a patient in the hall asks a question she can't answer, she finds somebody who can help.
- Pitches in with menial tasks, like filing or emptying bedpans, even if they're not in his job description. He doesn't regard them as thrilling, but he also knows what happens when they're neglected.

NURSING: A MOST VERSATILE PROFESSION

Jennifer Jacoby started as a nurse's aide, and became a licensed vocational nurse. "I loved the personal involvement with patients and the constant learning," she recalls.

Her determination to pursue a health care career doubled when she found a way to combine it with her passion for travel. "I learned that a nurse could always get a job anywhere," she says. After earning her bachelor's degree in nursing, Jacoby worked in three countries and seven different states.

"It's the most versatile of professions," she continues. "If you have a family and you need part-time work or flexible hours, it's there." As a nurse, you can work in schools, state or county health departments and corporations as well as hospitals and doctors' offices. "You can go into management or teaching," adds Jacoby who now has her master's degree in nursing and works as chief nursing officer at a hospital in San Diego.

Yes, it's hard work, she admits. "And I've even had days when I wished I had never gone to work," she says, "but there's never been a day when I was sorry I had become a nurse."

PERSONAL PROFILE

Michelle Groves
Certified Pharmacy Technician

Since the subject of pharmacy had always intrigued her, it was the logical choice when Michelle enrolled at the San Antonio College of Medical and Dental Assistants, in San Antonio, Texas. She earned her certificate as a pharmacy technician in 2001.

Michelle, 32, chose health care after serving in the military and working in the personal fitness industry. She placed one condition on her career however. "I didn't want hands-on work with patients. Handling bodily fluids was not something I wanted to do."

What Michelle Loves Most about Her Work

She sees a steady stream of patients at the walk-in pharmacy in a military hospital. "I love talking with them and knowing I'm doing something to make them feel better." The most trying moments come when she has to turn away someone who is not an ideal candidate for a drug. Even more difficult is saying no to a person who's not insured and can't afford to buy medicine out of pocket. "But 90 percent of the job is rewarding. That's what keeps me going," she says.

How Michelle Landed Her First-Choice Position

Early in her training, Michelle looked at the externship and job options for pharmacy technicians. It took no time to see that the hospital pharmacy was the best opportunity. It offered better career advancement prospects and paid seven to eight dollars an hour more than the retail pharmacies.

The catch was the difficulty of landing an externship at the hospital. She applied anyway and passed on several retail placements, assuring her counselors that the hospital opening would come around. Sure enough, it did. And a job offer followed before Michelle finished her training. "I worked hard for it all through my program," she admits. "I never studied so much in my life. I knew exactly what I wanted!"

The moral here is to do your research and choose the companies you want to work for, Michelle suggests. Look at the hours and the advancement opportunities, as well as salaries. "If it's something you want, strive for it. It could take more than one try, but keep your eye on the goal, and you'll get it," she says.

Once you get through the door, don't slack off, she warns. For Michelle, the old habits from school live on in her professional life. She still researches medications after hours and gets to work on time every day.

What Michelle Wishes She Had Known Earlier

"I wish I'd done it sooner!" she says. "I spent 15 years of my life enjoying my work less, thinking less of myself and making less money than if I'd gone in after high school." When asked to describe the most valuable aspect of her training, she says, "It gave me an incredible amount of self-confidence—something I never had before. It gave me a career in a short amount of time. It's what I need for the future."

WANT TO LEARN MORE?

Besides the resources listed with each occupation above, the following general sources may also be helpful:

- For referrals to the human resource departments in hospitals nationwide:

  American Hospital Association
  Phone: (312) 422-3000
  Website: www.aha.org

- For details on educational programs for health occupations, ask your librarian for the *Health Professions Career and Education Directory* (HPCED) or go to the AMA's website for medical education resources:

  American Medical Association
  Website: www.ama-assn.org/ama/pub/category/4847.html

- The U.S. Bureau of Labor Statistics offers resources galore through its huge website. For general career information, visit www.bls.gov, click on the Occupational Outlook Handbook and find the "Career Information" link. From there you can link to special sites for workers with disabilities, older workers, and women, for example.

- This book of 21 interviews with health care workers provides first-hand scenarios from the field. *Real People Working in Health Care*, by Blythe Camenson (1997, VGM Career Horizons, Lincolnwood).

- If your dream is to travel and earn as you go, check with American Traveler Staffing Professionals, which places allied health professionals in hospitals and health care organizations nationwide. Assignments last from two months to two years.

  American Traveler Staffing Professionals
  Phone: (800) 884-8788
  Website: www.americantraveler.net

- To glean direct insights from professionals in the field, check out the nursing discussion groups at www.acad.sunytccc.edu/nursing/sn.html. Locate similar discussion groups for other occupations through a search engine like Google or Dogpile. As key words, use the title of the occupation, such as "occupational therapy" and "discussion group" or "news group" or "listserv."

Chapter Three

CAREER CLOSE-UPS

Some people go into health careers through the "front door," straight out of high school. But there are side doors, too—through the fitness industry, fast food, construction, or military service, for example. Whether it's jumping in right out of high school, or waiting as long as 20 years, there is no "one" way to meet your career goals in health care.

Some health workers have clinical jobs; others rarely see patients. But at the end of the day, they all have one thing in common: "No matter what health career you're in, each and every thing you do can make someone better—or it can make them worse. People rely on you to know your job and to take pride in doing it well," states Michelle Groves, C.Ph.T., a certified pharmacy technician in a Texas hospital. "If I make a mistake on one prescription, someone's life could be at stake!"

The career close-ups that follow will give you a better understanding of jobs like that of Michelle Groves, and a fuller idea of what they require. You'll also see what they mean when they say that health care has jobs to satisfy any interest.

Each close-up includes a "career ladder" listing, just a few of the directions you could take to broaden your job responsibilities and increase your income. Most career ladder steps require further education. Seven of the occupations appear on the U.S. Bureau of Labor Statistics' list of 30 "Hot Jobs"—the fastest growing occupations through 2008.

1. Dental Assistant

Ranked # 18 of 30 Hot Jobs

Projected growth through 2008: 42 percent

Number of jobs by 2008: 325,000

Salary: $7.00 to $16.00 an hour

Job Outlook

- Younger dentists, unlike their senior colleagues, usually hire one or two dental assistants. That accounts for some of the growth in this occupation.
- Numerous jobs will open up as today's dental assistants take advanced training and move into higher paying jobs.

Practice Settings

- Private dental offices (97 percent)
- Dental schools, hospitals, public health departments or clinics (3 percent)

Profile of a Dental Assistant

Personality Traits: Accurate, careful, cheerful, compassionate, cooperative, efficient, gentle, punctual, tolerant

Skills: Anticipate needs of others, follow instruction, learn by listening, nurture people, organize objects, tasks, and schedules

Job Setting: Business side of health care, different patients each day, direct patient care, manual work with equipment/machines, quiet surroundings, regular hours, work with adults, work with children

Learning to Be a Dental Assistant

- Length of training: Certificate or diploma: one year or less; associate's degree: two years
- Prerequisite: High school or GED (high school equivalency certificate)
- Course work: Dental assisting techniques, basic anatomy of the mouth and head, and dental office practice skills.

- Field experience or externship: Dental clinics and private offices
- Accredited programs: Over 250 in community colleges, trade schools, technical institutes, or the military.
- Certification and credentials: Certification is available through the Dental Assisting National Board. Several states have certification exams for dental assistants whose duties involve shooting and developing X rays.

What Dental Assisting is Really Like

Dental assistants may have responsibilities for patient care, office work, and laboratory procedures. At the chair side, they assist dentists with exams and treatments, handing them instruments as necessary. They prepare and assist patients before and during dental procedures. Some shoot and develop dental X rays, remove sutures and apply anesthetics to the gums.

Those with lab duties make casts of the teeth and mouth from impressions taken by dentists. They clean and polish dental appliances and make temporary crowns. In the office, they might schedule appointments, handle billing, keep the books and order supplies.

What You Need to Succeed as a Dental Assistant

Dental assistants need manual dexterity to handle suction devices and cotton swabs within the confined space of a patient's mouth. In the lab, you will work with delicate dental appliances and operate sophisticated equipment. At the chair side, you will be the dentist's "third hand." The work requires an ability to follow directions, to focus on the treatment, and even to anticipate ways to streamline the experience for the patient and dentist alike.

The Inside Scoop on Dental Assistants

Female dental assistants will find more job opportunities than male assistants, explains dental clinic manager, Roland Cutting who started as a dental technologist in the military. "Male dentists are just more likely to hire female dental assistants, except in the military or in large dental organizations," he explains.

Career Ladder for Dental Assistants
- Dental hygienist
- Dentist
- Dental clinic manager
- Sales representative for dental products
- Dental insurance claims processor

To Learn More
- For career opportunities, scholarships, accredited dental assistant programs, and certification requirements:

  Commission on Dental Accreditation
  American Dental Association
  Phone: (312) 440-2718
  Website: www.ada.org/prof/ed/index.asp
  Dental Assisting National Board, Inc.
  Phone: (312) 642-3368
  Website: www.danb.org

- For career opportunities, training and continuing education:

  American Dental Assistants Association
  Phone: (312) 541-1550
  Website: www.dentalassist.org
  National Association of Health Career Schools
  Phone: (202) 842-1592
  Website: www.nahcs.org

2. Health Information Technician

Ranked #14 of 30 Hot Jobs
Projected growth through 2008: 44 percent
Number of jobs by 2008: 133,000
Salary $18,000 to $26,000

Career Close-Ups

Job Outlook
- The number of openings will outnumber the available workers. The expansion is driven by higher numbers of medical tests and procedures that come under close scrutiny by insurance companies, governmental agencies, courts and consumers.
- Excellent opportunities are available for medical records coders, a closely related and relatively new health information specialty.
- In addition to hospitals—the traditional employers of medical records specialists—opportunities will rise in medical offices, clinics, nursing homes and home health agencies.

Practice Settings
- Hospitals (40 percent)
- Nursing homes, medical offices and clinics, and home health agencies (55 percent)
- Public health departments (3 percent)
- Insurance companies (2 percent)

Profile of a Health Information Technician

Personality traits: Accurate, analytical, attentive to detail, careful, curious, organized, thorough

Skills: Communicate well in writing, follow instruction, learn by reading, organize tasks and schedules, research facts and figures, type accurately, work with technical data

Job setting: Business side of health care, desk job, flexible hours, job security, quiet surroundings

Learning to Be a Health Information Technician
- Length of training: Two years or less
- Prerequisite: High school diploma or GED
- Helpful background: High school biology, chemistry, health and computer courses

43

Career Close-Ups

- Course work: Overview of the health care industry, medical terminology, anatomy and physiology, legal aspects of health information, coding and abstraction of data, statistics, database management, health care quality improvement methods and computer training.
- Accredited programs: Around 170 in vocational schools and community colleges.
- Certification and credentials: Health information technician graduates pass an exam to earn the credential Accredited Record Technician (ART).

What Health Information Technology is Really Like

Health information or medical records technicians work with patient records or charts made by health care providers. They organize and evaluate the documents for accuracy and completeness. The work requires an understanding of medical practices and familiarity with computers and health-related software programs, as they must enter data into the computer. Technicians often talk with physicians to clarify a diagnosis or obtain additional information.

Health information technicians are responsible for coding each diagnosis and procedure in the record. Coding is based on an intricate set of diagnosis-related groups (DRG) for inpatient care and other coding systems for outpatient care. To a great extent, coding determines how much insurance companies and government programs pay on the claims submitted by health care providers. Since medical records often become critical in court cases and insurance appeals, codes must be accurate with supportive documents on file.

Health information technicians process statistical data, the backbone of numerous reports that health care organizations submit to governmental agencies and insurance companies. Typical reports include the average number of days patients are hospitalized for pneumonia or cardiac surgery, or the numbers of births and deaths. Besides routine reports, there are special surveys for research projects and public relations campaigns.

Tumor registrars are health information specialists who compile and maintain the records of cancer patients for use by physicians and medical researchers.

What You Need to Succeed as a Health Information Technician

Health information technology is one of the few health care occupations with little or no direct patient contact. If you love to take various loose ends and transform them into something useful, this could be the job for you. The type of person who prefers to work behind the scenes would do best in this career. Success depends on accuracy with details and organizational skills.

The Inside Scoop on Health Information Technology

These jobs usually involve 40-hour work weeks without much overtime. In hospitals where medical records departments are open 18 to 24 hours a day, the work week may include overtime. After regular eight-to-five business hours, health information technicians fulfill requests for medical records from emergency departments. They also pull records for the following day's clinics or surgical patients.

Coders need a good grasp on diseases and medical procedures to pinpoint the appropriate code for each case. It's more than simply looking up a certain medical test in the code list. For example, treating pneumonia in an otherwise healthy 21-year-old will entail fewer costs than treating pneumonia in a 65-year-old with heart problems and diabetes.

Health information technicians face some job hazards. They spend long hours at the computer, and must protect themselves against eye strain and wrist injuries.

Career Ladder for Health Information Technicians

- Coding specialist
- Medical records section supervisor
- Department or project manager
- Senior technician
- Health information administrator

To Learn More

- For career information and a list of accredited training programs:
  American Health Information Management Association
  Phone: (312) 233-1100
  Website: www.ahima.org
  Email: info@ahima.org

Career Close-Ups

3. Licensed Practical Nurse (L.P.N.)
Projected growth through 2008: 15 percent
Number of jobs by 2008: 795,800
Salary: $20,000 to $37,000

Job Outlook
- Most L.P.N. jobs will be in long-term care such as assisted living facilities and nursing homes. Hospitals will hire fewer L.P.N.s because the number of inpatients needing L.P.N.-level skills is not expected to increase much.
- L.P.N.s will work primarily with elderly patients who need assistance with their daily living activities and basic care for chronic illnesses such as diabetes or heart problems.
- As more complex health care procedures are shifted to home environments, home health care agencies will hire more L.P.N.s. In fact, the Bureau of Labor Statistics predicts growth of at least 36 percent in home health jobs for L.P.N.s.
- About 25 percent of L.P.N.s work part time.

Practice Settings
- Hospitals (32 percent)
- Nursing homes (28 percent)
- Doctors' offices and clinics (14 percent)
- Temporary help agencies, home health care, residential care facilities (such as assisted living), schools or government agencies (26 percent)

Profile of an L.P.N.
Personality traits: Calm, dependable, friendly, gentle, hard-working, punctual, tolerant

Skills: Communicate well in a one-to-one setting, cope with interruptions, listen attentively, nurture people, observe behavior changes

Job setting: Different patients each day, direct patient care, fast pace, flexible hours, physical activity, regular hours, work with adults, work with children

Learning to Be an L.P.N.

- Length of training: One year or less for state license
- Prerequisite: High school diploma
- Course work: Anatomy, physiology, medical-surgical nursing, pediatrics (care of children), obstetrics (labor and delivery), psychiatric nursing (mental health), nutrition, first aid and administration of drugs
- Clinical practice or externship: Mostly in hospitals
- Accredited programs: 1,100 mostly in technical and vocational schools, with a few in community colleges, high schools, hospitals, or colleges
- Certification and credentials: All states require a licensing exam after graduation. In Texas and California, passage results in the Licensed Vocational Nurse (L.V.N.) credential. In all other states, it's L.P.N.

What an L.P.N.'s Work is Really Like

This is bedside care in the true sense of the word. L.P.N.s take vital signs, give injections, massages, enemas. They apply ice packs, give massages and administer medications. They bathe and feed patients and attend to their emotional needs. More experienced L.P.N.s develop care plans, supervise nursing assistants and aides.

In doctors' offices, L.P.N.s keep records, make appointments and do some clerical tasks. In private homes, they prepare meals for patients and teach families simple nursing procedures.

What You Need to Succeed as an L.P.N.

In the last chapter we mentioned how a lot of health care amounts to quiet, routine work: L.P.N.s do a lot of that. The ones who excel at their jobs know how much little things mean to a sick person—kind words to ease the embarrassment after a bed wetting accident, for example. A good L.P.N. can comfort a family whose loved one is dying of AIDS. As part of the health care team, these nurses implement care plans and report patients' progress to other care givers.

Career Close-Ups

The Inside Scoop on L.P.N.s

This can be a high-stress job. It involves a great deal of standing, walking, and helping patients move from bed to wheelchair. The job hazards include exposure to radiation or infectious diseases such as hepatitis and sometimes back problems. The workloads are often heavy. The patients can be confused, frightened, irrational, or uncooperative. L.P.N.s need to be sympathetic and firm. In spite of the pressure, they must strictly observe safety precautions to protect themselves and their patients from unnecessary exposure to radiation or infectious diseases.

Terrie Waters Dunlap, an L.V.N. in Imperial Beach, California puts it this way: "It can be the most rewarding *and* the most heartbreaking career you will ever have. It's rewarding to help someone who's very ill get better. And it's hard to lose someone when you become attached to them. I love my elderly patients and it's sad to see them pass away. Still, it is rewarding to know that I've helped ease them through the last days of their lives."

Career Ladder for L.P.N.s

- Registered nurse with associate's degree
- Registered nurse with bachelor's degree

To Learn More

- For career opportunities and training:

    National League for Nursing
    Phone: (212) 363-5555; (800) 669-1665
    Website: www.nln.org

    National Association for Practical Nurse Education and Service
    Phone: (301) 588-2491
    Website: www.napnes.org
    Email: napnes@bellatlantic.net

4. Medical Assistant

Ranked #8 of 30 Hot Jobs

Projected growth through 2008: 58 percent

Number of jobs by 2008: 398,000

Salary: $15,000 to $28,000

Job Outlook

- Though some medical assistants earn the title through on-the-job training, job opportunities are best for those with formal training and certification.
- The demand for medical assistants is driven by the growth in medical group practices, clinics, and other health care facilities that need well-trained support staff.

Practice Settings

- Doctors' offices (65 percent)
- Health practitioners' office, including chiropractors, optometrists, and podiatrists (14 percent)
- Hospitals, nursing homes and other health care facilities (21 percent)

Profile of a Medical Assistant

Personality traits: Accurate, attentive to detail, calm, cheerful, compassionate, considerate, dependable, efficient, patient, self-confident, tactful, thorough, tolerant

Skills: Anticipate needs of others, communicate in a one-to-one setting and by telephone, cope with interruptions, get along with people, learn by reading, nurture people, organize tasks, and schedules

Job setting: Desk job on the business side of health care, different patients each day, direct patient care, job description can be flexible, job security, people contact, excluding hands-on care, physical activity, work with adults, work with children

Career Close-Ups

Learning to be a Medical Assistant
- Length of training: One year for certificate or diploma; two years for associate's degree
- Prerequisite: Applicants usually need a high school diploma or GED
- Helpful background: High school courses in math, health, biology, typing, bookkeeping, computers, and office skills. Volunteer experience in health care.
- Course work: Anatomy, physiology, medical terminology, typing, transcription, record keeping, accounting, insurance processing, lab techniques, clinical and diagnostic procedures, pharmaceutical principles, medication administration, first aid, health care office practices, patient relations, medical law and ethics
- Field experience or externship: Physicians' offices, hospitals or other health care facilities
- Accredited programs: Approximately 600 in vocational schools, community colleges, and universities
- Certification and credentials: Medical Assistants take a national exam to earn one of three equally recognized credentials: Certified Medical Assistant, Registered Medical Assistant or Podiatric Medical Assistant Certified. The credentials are awarded by three different organizations listed below.

What Medical Assisting is Really Like

Medical assistants keep the office running smoothly. They handle routine administrative and clinical tasks. In small practices, medical assistants are "generalists," with administrative duties in the front office and clinical in the back. In large practices, they specialize in one area or the other.

Administrative duties may include answering phones, greeting patients, updating patient records, filling out insurance forms, handling correspondence, arranging hospital admissions or lab services, as well as billing and bookkeeping.

Clinical duties vary according to state law. Typically they include taking medical histories and vital signs, explaining treatment procedures to patients, and assisting physicians during examinations. Medical assistants also collect and prepare lab specimens and do basic lab tests. They may instruct patients about medication or special diets. Other responsibilities might include electrocardiograms (EKGs), removing sutures, and changing dressings.

Podiatric medical assistants make castings of feet, shoot and develop X rays, and assist podiatrists in surgery.

Ophthalmic (eye care) medical assistants help ophthalmologists with diagnostic tests and surgery. They also show patients how to use contact lenses, eye dressings and protective eye gear.

What You Need to Succeed as a Medical Assistant

Compassion, courtesy, and friendliness are essential. There's a good deal of contact with patients. These professionals must be able to communicate doctors' instructions and calm patients' nerves. They must respect the confidentiality of medical information.

Attention to detail is also critical, whether it means accurate filing, setting out the right instruments for an exam, or precise recording of vital signs.

The Inside Scoop on Medical Assisting

"This is one of the best careers in health care," observes Loyda Morales, a registered medical assistant in a small medical office in San Antonio. "It helps you to help others," she adds, "and it gives you constant opportunities to learn." If you're not sure exactly which health care specialty you'd like to pursue, "medical assisting is a good way to get your feet wet. It lets you try out different things instead of going into something blindly and finding out you don't like it."

Career Ladder for Medical Assistants

- Nurse
- Medical office manager
- Medical technologist
- Health information specialist
- Physician assistant
- Respiratory therapist

Career Close-Ups

To Learn More:

- For career opportunities and the Certified Medical Assistant exam:
  American Association of Medical Assistants
  Phone: (312) 899-1500
  Website: www.aama-ntl.org

- For career opportunities and the Registered Medical Assistant exam:
  American Medical Technologists
  Phone: (847) 823-5169
  Website: www.amt1.com
  Email: mail@amt1.com

- For careers and certification for podiatric assistants:
  American Society of Podiatric Medical Assistants
  Phone: (708) 863-6303; (888) 882-7762
  Website: www.aspma.org
  Email: SandraPMAC@aol.com

- For careers, training and the Certified Ophthalmic Assistant exam:
  Joint Commission on Allied Health Personnel in Ophthalmology
  Phone: (651) 731-2944; (800) 284-3937
  Website: www.jcahpo.org
  Email: jcahpo@jcahpo.org

- For ABHES-accredited programs:
  Accrediting Bureau of Health Education Schools (ABHES)
  Phone: (703) 533-2082
  Website: www.abhes.org
  Email: info@abhes.org

- For training programs and career information:
  National Association of Health Career Schools
  Phone: (202) 842-1592
  Website: www.nahcs.org

5. Occupational Therapy (OT) Assistants and Aides

Ranked #22 of 30 Hot Jobs

Projected growth through 2008: 40 percent

Number of jobs: 26,000

Salary: $15,000 to $45,000 (assistants earn less than aides)

Job Outlook

A growing population of elderly will increase the demand for OT assistants and aides. These professionals play key roles in rehabilitating stroke victims and arthritis sufferers. Among all age groups, more patients are surviving critical health problems and need rehabilitation.

Practice Settings

- Occupational therapy offices (40 percent)
- Hospitals (30 percent)
- Nursing homes, doctors' offices, social service agencies, outpatient rehabilitation centers and home health agencies (30 percent)

Profile of an OT Assistant or Aide

Personality traits: Attentive to detail, compassionate, considerate, dependable, gentle, punctual, tactful, tolerant

Skills: Communicate in a one-to-one setting, follow instruction, get along with people, nurture people, observe behavior changes, organize tasks and schedules, repair machines and other objects, teach adults, teach children

Job Setting: Different patients each day, direct patient care, manual work with equipment, machines, etc., people contact excluding hands-on care, physical activity, regular hours

Learning to be an OT Assistant or Aide

Length of training: 12 to 18 months for a certificate; two years for an associate's degree. OT aides receive most of their training on the job.

Career Close-Ups

Helpful background: High school courses in biology and health, as well as volunteer work in nursing homes, occupational or physical therapy offices, or other health care facilities

Course work: Introduction to health care, basic medical terminology, anatomy, physiology, and occupational therapy techniques

Field experience or externship: Mental health agencies, pediatrics, elder care facilities, or other health facilities

Accredited programs: Over 165 programs in community colleges and technical schools

Certification and credentials: Graduates pass a national certification exam to earn the credential of certified occupational therapy assistant.

What the Work of OT Assistants and Aides is Really Like

The goal of OT is to help people compensate for impairments from physical or mental disorders. OT workers help patients develop skills they can use in the job market or to increase their independence in tasks like preparing meals or using public transportation. OT assistants and aides work under the direction of occupational therapists.

OT assistants help clients with rehab activities as outlined by an occupational therapist: They might teach patients how to move safely from a wheelchair to a bed, or how to stretch and strengthen an injured hand. These professionals must be comfortable monitoring and coaxing patients so that they do their exercises correctly. They record progress, and discuss treatment plans and progress with the occupational therapist, and fill out insurance billing forms.

OT aides are less involved in direct patient care, as they typically prepare materials and equipment for treatment. They also handle support tasks such as scheduling appointments, answering phone calls, ordering supplies, and managing paperwork.

What You Need to Succeed as an OT Assistant or Aide

OT assistants and aides must feel comfortable working toward goals that have been set by others. It is the occupational therapist in charge who designs the patient's treatment plan, and the assistants and aides are there to support that plan. OT aides need a high tolerance for routine tasks that must be done accurately, such as taking phone messages, ordering supplies, and scheduling appointments.

Career Close-Ups

The Inside Scoop on OT Assistants and Aides

OT assistants have more varied responsibilities than do OT aides. The work involves many hours of standing and, at times, helping to lift patients or equipment. People in this field usually work regular business hours, with occasional weekends and evenings.

Career Ladder for OT Assistants
- Occupational therapist
- Physical therapist
- Rehabilitation clinic manager

Career Ladder for OT Aides
- OT assistant
- Occupational therapist
- Medical assistant

To Learn More
- For career information and a list of accredited programs:
  American Occupational Therapy Association
  Phone: (301) 652-2682
  Website: www.aota.org
  Email: educate@aota.org

6. Personal Care and Home Health Aide

Ranked # 7 of 30 Hot Jobs
Projected growth through 2008: 58 percent
Number of jobs: 1,179,000
Salary : $7.50 to $8.00 per hour

Job Outlook

Several trends drive the demand for personal care and home health aides. One is quite familiar by now: the rising number of senior adults needing help with personal care and daily activities. Health care practitioners are coming to recognize that patients of any age get well faster in their own familiar surroundings. Finally, advances in medical technology make it possible to shift ever more complicated treatments into the home setting.

Practice Settings
- Home health and personal care agencies
- Visiting nurse services
- Residential care facilities
- Hospitals
- Public health and welfare departments
- Community volunteer agencies
- Nursing and personal care facilities
- Temporary help firms
- Self-employment

Profile of a Personal Care and Home Health Aide

Personality traits: Attentive to detail, calm, considerate, compassionate, dependable, hard working, patient, tactful

Skills: Anticipate needs of others, communicate in a one-to-one setting, concentrate amid chaos, cope with interruptions, follow instructions, get along with people, listen attentively, nurture people, observe behavior changes

Job setting: Different patients each day, direct patient care, fast pace, flexible job description, flexible hours, job security, low turnover among patients, physical activity, work with adults, work with children

Learning to be a Personal Care and Home Health Aide

Length of training: 75 hours for a certificate

Skill training: In agencies receiving reimbursements from Medicare (federal government insurance for the elderly), home health and personal care aides pass a competency test covering 12 areas: (1) communication skills; (2) observation and reporting of patient status and the care provided; (3) reading vital signs; (4) basic infection control procedures; (5) basic body functions and changes that could indicate problems;

(6) maintenance of a clean, safe, healthy environment; (7) emergency procedures; (8) techniques for observing the physical, emotional and developmental characteristics of patients; (9) personal hygiene; (10) safe techniques for moving patients; (11) normal range of motion and body positions; (12) basic nutrition.

Field experience: Practical experience supervised by a registered nurse

Accredited programs: Currently, accreditation does not apply, as state laws vary widely and formal training is not a prerequisite for the federal competency exam.

Certification and credentials: The National Association for Home Care offers certification for personal care and home health aides who wish to demonstrate that they have met basic industry standards. Requirements for formal training vary by state. In some states, on-the-job training is enough. Some states require a physical exam, including a test for tuberculosis (TB). Federal law suggests, but does not require, at least 75 hours of classroom instruction and practical training supervised by a registered nurse.

What the Work of Personal Care and Home Health Aides is Really Like

The work of personal care and home health aides enables thousands of elderly, disabled, and ill persons to live in their own homes instead of health care institutions. Some aides care for the small children whose parent is incapacitated. Others help recently discharged hospital patients with short-term needs.

Home health aides provide health-related services such as administering oral medications. Other duties include checking temperature, pulse and breathing rates, giving massages or assisting with braces and artificial limbs.

Personal care and *home care aides* provide mainly housekeeping and routine personal care services. But duties among the specialties often overlap and vary according to agency policies. Both types of aides do some housekeeping as well as personal care, whether it's cleaning the house, doing laundry, or changing bed linens. Some aides plan meals, including special diets for diabetics or for Parkinson's disease patients who can't swallow solid foods, and some take clients shopping or to medical appointments.

Home health and personal care aides instruct or provide emotional support for their clients. They might assist in toilet training a severely mentally handicapped child or simply listen to a client who needs a sympathetic ear.

In home care agencies, these caregivers work under the supervision of registered nurses, physical therapists or social workers. They participate in case reviews, and generally, make client visits on their own. Sometimes they'll go to the same home every day for months, but usually they see four to five clients a day for short-term needs. They're regarded as team members along with the registered nurses, therapists and social workers.

What You Need to Succeed as a Personal Care or Home Health Aide

Access to a car is practically a necessity because of the travel involved. A good aide likes to help people with their most basic needs and understands that illness can make "difficult personalities" out of the nicest people. The work is hard physically and emotionally. It requires compassion and a cheerful disposition. Tact, honesty, and discretion are critical because aides work in people's homes.

The Inside Scoop on Personal Care and Home Health Aides

These workers see it all, from well-kept, happy homes to disheveled, depressing homes. Some clients are angry and uncooperative; others are pleasant and appreciative.

Turnover is high in this occupation because the work is hard and the pay is low. But on a positive note, it serves as a doorway into health care. There are many openings. You can work flexible hours and pick up great experience while you train to advance your career.

Career Ladder for Personal Care and Home Health Aides

- Licensed practical nurse
- Registered nurse
- Physical, occupational or respiratory therapy aide
- Medical assistant
- Health information technician

To Learn More

- For referrals to state and local job opportunities, as well as a list of publications and information on national certification:

  National Association for Home Care
  Phone: (202) 547-7424

Website: www.nahc.org
Email: research@nahc.org

- For career and training information:
National Association of Health Career Schools
Phone: (202) 842-1565
Website: www.nahcs.org

7. Pharmacy Technician and Assistant

Projected growth through 2008: 15 percent
Number of jobs by 2008: 196,000
Salary: $7.00 to $13.00 an hour

Job Outlook

As the pharmaceutical branch of health care expands, so does the need for pharmacy technicians and assistants. Medications are an increasingly important part of medical practice. And the heaviest users of medications are the elderly, who generally need the most health services.

Job opportunities will be better for pharmacy technicians and assistants with formal training or previous experience than for those who need on-the-job training.

Practice Settings

- Retail pharmacies (70 percent)
- Hospitals (20 percent)
- Mail-order pharmacies, clinics, pharmaceutical wholesalers and federal government agencies (10 percent)

Profile of a Pharmacy Assistant

Personality: Accurate, analytical, attentive to detail, efficient, punctual, thorough

Skills: Communicate by phone and in writing, cope with interruptions, follow instruction, learn by reading, listen attentively, organize supplies and work equipment, work with technical data and numbers

Career Close-Ups

Job setting: Flexible hours, job security, manual work with equipment/machines, people contact (excluding hands-on care), regular hours

Learning to be a Pharmacy Technician or Assistant

Length of training: On the job for pharmacy assistant; one year or less for pharmacy technician

Prerequisite: High school diploma or GED

Classroom and lab work: Medical and pharmaceutical terminology; pharmaceutical calculations and techniques; pharmacy record keeping, laws and ethics; and medication uses and doses

Field experience or externship: Retail or hospital pharmacies

Accredited programs: Currently, there are few state and no federal requirements for formal training of pharmacy technicians, so accreditation does not apply. In response to the growing demand for formally trained pharmacy technicians, however, more vocational schools and community colleges are offering courses.

Certification and credentials: The Pharmacy Technician Certification Board offers the National Pharmacy Technician Certification Examination. Those who pass the exam become Certified Pharmacy Technician (C.Ph.T.). Although certification is still voluntary, more than half of the pharmacy technicians in the United States are certified.

What the Work of a Pharmacy Technician and Assistant is Really Like

Pharmacy technicians have more complex tasks than do assistants. Technicians count and label prescribed medications. Other responsibilities vary according to the work setting:

Retail pharmacy technicians verify the accuracy of written prescriptions and refill requests. They package medications and print out instructions from pharmacy databases. The pharmacist signs off on each medication that leaves the pharmacy.

Technicians also maintain computerized patient drug profiles and file insurance claim forms. Other duties might include stocking and inventorying prescription and over-the-counter drugs, and maintaining pharmacy equipment.

Hospital pharmacy technicians read patients' charts, prepare, and deliver medicine to the patient care units. Some deliveries are 24-hour supplies, or one-time doses for special treatments or for the emergency department. Technicians also keep inventories of drugs, chemicals, and other supplies. The pharmacist supervises and signs off on the technician's work.

Pharmacy assistants have less responsibility for medications. Their work often involves answering the telephone, stocking shelves, and clerical work.

What you Need to Succeed as a Pharmacy Technician or Assistant

This work takes a good deal of stamina because it involves hours on your feet, lifting heavy boxes of supplies, and climbing stepladders to pull items from high shelves. The job entails 35- to 40-hour work weeks, with a fair share of evening, weekend, and holiday work in hospitals and retail stores. There are plenty of part-time jobs.

Good customer service and communication skills are essential. Technicians must be adept at reading, spelling, and basic computer operation. Accuracy in measuring and counting are critical—and sometimes a matter of life and death. Although pharmacists check the prescriptions, technicians would be grossly negligent if they relied on that instead of carefully monitoring the quality of their own work.

The Inside Scoop on Pharmacy Technicians and Assistants

Pharmacy assistants must be accurate and efficient in handling repetitious tasks like taking phone messages and operating a cash register.

Pharmacy technicians need to master new technologies as they come along. For example, more and more pharmacies are using robotic machines to put medications into containers and technicians have to learn how to stock and program the machines. Instead of eliminating the need for technicians, this shift will rewrite their job descriptions.

"If you love dealing with people, but do not want to do hands-on care, this is a good health care job," observes Michelle Groves, C.Ph.T., a military hospital pharmacy technician in Converse, Texas. She offers another insight on formal schooling versus on-the-job training: While some retail pharmacies promise earnings while you learn on the job, the opportunities for advancement are next to zero. And without formal training, Groves adds, it's nearly impossible to work in a hospital pharmacy—where the pay and advancement opportunities are better.

Career Close-Ups

Career Ladder for Pharmacy Assistants
- Pharmacy technician
- Registered pharmacist

Career Ladder for Pharmacy Technicians
- Specialist in nuclear medicine, e.g., the radioactive dyes used in diagnostic tests
- Specialist in chemotherapy drugs for cancer treatment
- Sales representative for a pharmaceutical company
- Registered pharmacist

To Learn More
- For certification and PTCB Exam Information:

    Pharmacy Technician Certification Board
    Phone: (202) 429-7576
    Website: www.ptcb.org
    Email: PTCBinfo@ptcb.org

- For career information:

    American Society of Health System Pharmacists
    Phone: (301) 657-3000
    Website: www.ashp.org
    Email: www@ashp.org

    National Association of Chain Drug Stores
    Phone: (703) 549-3001
    Website: www.nacds.org
    Email: pharmacy_affairs@nacds.org

8. Physical Therapy (PT) Assistant/Aide

Ranked #15 of 30 Hot Jobs

Projected growth through 2008: 44 percent

Number of jobs by 2008: 118,000

Salary $13,000 to $39,000 (PT assistants earn more than PT aides)

Job Outlook

PT will become more important as the elderly population grows; it is a critical part of rehabilitation following heart attacks, strokes, and hip replacements. Medical advances that increase the survival odds among serious trauma victims will also drive the demand for PT services.

Practice Settings

- Hospitals and PT offices (70 percent)
- Nursing facilities, rehabilitation centers, physicians' offices/clinics, and home health agencies (30 percent)

Profile of a PT Aide or Assistant

Personality traits: Attentive to detail, careful, cheerful, compassionate, dependable, friendly, gentle, patient, tactful, tolerant

Skills: Communicate in a one-to-one setting and in writing, follow instruction, get along with people, learn by observing, organize work equipment, repair machines, teach adults, teach children

Job setting: Different patients each day, direct patient care, flexible hours, manual work with equipment, physical activity, quiet surroundings, regular hours, work with adults, work with children

Learning to Be a PT Aide or Assistant

PT aides are trained on the job, while *PT assistants'* take formal training

Length of training: Two years or less. Admission into PT assistant programs is competitive; long waiting lists are common.

Course work: Algebra, anatomy and physiology, biology, chemistry, psychology, cardiopulmonary resuscitation (CPR), and basic first aid.

Field experience: Hospitals, rehabilitation centers, PT offices and home health agencies

Accredited programs: Approximately 275 in vocational schools, community colleges and universities.

Certification and credentials: PT assistants graduate with an associate's degree. Most states require graduates to pass a licensure exam.

What the Work of PT Aides and Assistants is Really Like

These professionals implement procedures delegated by a supervising physical therapist. The patients come for pain relief and rehabilitation from injuries or conditions such as arthritis or cerebral palsy.

PT assistants help patients do special strength-building or joint movement exercises, provide massages, electrical stimulation, hot and cold packs, traction, and ultrasound. They record patient progress and have case conferences with the physical therapist.

PT aides provide support services such as cleaning treatment areas and preparing the patients for therapy. At times they help move patients or give them a shoulder to lean on during exercises. In some settings, aides order supplies, answer phones, and handle paperwork.

What You Need to Succeed as a PT Assistant or Aide

Physical therapy takes a moderate amount of physical stamina because the work involves constant kneeling, stooping, bending and standing. Many patients have to be lifted due to loss of mobility. PT assistants often act as coach or cheerleader: They must encourage patients regularly, and teach them correct exercise techniques to avoid injury. The most successful professionals have a keen eye for modifications in therapy routines to suit specific patient needs.

The Inside Scoop on PT Assistants and Aides

Physical therapy professionals must be diplomatic in the area of pushing patients toward their goals. If a patient chooses not to carry out the rehab exercises, a skilled professional will know when to push and when to back off. At the other extreme, if a patient holds out unrealistic expectations for recovery, a good PT professional will gently explain the outlook for recovery while not squashing the patient's enthusiasm. After all, that enthusiasm could be exactly what the patient needs to beat the odds!

Career Ladder for PT Assistants
- Physical therapist

Career Ladder for PT Aides
- PT assistant
- Physical therapist

To Learn More
- For career information and a list of schools offering accredited programs:

    American Physical Therapy Association
    Phone: (703) 684-2782; (800) 999-2782
    Website: www.apta.org
    Email: education@apta.org

- For state licensure requirements, see your local phone directory, state government listings, department of regulatory agencies

9. Radiologic Technologist

Projected growth through 2008: 15 percent
Number of jobs by 2008: 186,500
Salary: $24,000 to $48,000

Job Outlook
Radiologic technologists with formal education and cross training in nuclear medicine or another diagnostic technology have the best prospects. At present, hospitals are the principal job source for radiologic technologists. Due to the shift toward outpatient care, though, the highest rate of new job growth is in doctors' offices, clinics and diagnostic imaging centers. In hospitals, multiskilled employees will be the most sought after. About 20 percent of radiologic technologists work part time.

Practice Settings
- Hospitals (60 percent)
- Physicians' offices, clinics and diagnostic imaging centers (40 percent)

Profile of a Radiologic Technologist

Personality traits: Accurate, analytical, attentive to detail, calm, gentle, punctual, tactful, thorough

Skills: Communicate in one-to-one setting and in writing, learn by observing, learn by reading, organize work equipment, repair machines, work with technical data, work with numbers

Job setting: Different patients each day, job security, manual work with equipment, physical activity, regular hours, work with adults, work with children

Learning to Be a Radiologic Technologist

Length of training: Two years for an associate's degree (most popular option); four years for a bachelor's degree; one year for a certificate (for experienced radiographers or individuals from other health occupations such as medical technology or nursing)

Prerequisite: High school diploma or GED

Helpful background: High school math, physics, chemistry, and biology

Course work: Anatomy and physiology, patient care procedures, radiation physics, radiation protection, medical terminology, medical ethics, radiobiology, and pathology

Accredited programs: Around 605 radiography programs and 80 sonography programs in hospitals, colleges and universities, technical institutes, and the military

Certification and credentials: Most states require radiologic technologists to be licensed. However, no states require sonographers to be licensed. In both occupations, certification (or registration) is voluntary. Requirements include graduation from an accredited program and passing a national exam.

What Radiologic Technology is Really Like

The most familiar use of X-ray technology is diagnosing broken bones, but it is also used to diagnose tumors, clogged blood vessels, and many other ailments. It's also a treatment for cancer, where radiation is beamed directly into tumors. Other cancer treatments involve implanting small chips of radioactive material near tumors to stop the spread. Computerized tomography scanners (CT or CAT scans) produce cross sectional views of patients.

In addition to medical imaging with X rays, two other techniques are coming into more frequent use: Ultrasound and magnetic resonance imaging (MRI). All of the techniques come under the general title of radiologic technology.

The practice of radiologic technology is divided into two specialties:

(1) *Radiographers* produce X-ray films (radiographs) for diagnosing medical problems. The process includes preparing patients by explaining procedures and positioning them for the procedure, setting controls on the imaging machine, and finally, shooting the picture and developing the film. Throughout the procedure, radiographers use lead shields to prevent unnecessary exposure to radiation. Experienced radiographers do the more complex tests such as fluoroscopies, in which the patient drinks a solution that colors body tissues for imaging.

Radiographers might specialize or cross train as *CT technologists*, operating computerized tomography scanners, or *MRI technologists*, operating machines that use giant magnets and radio waves rather than radiation to create images of the body.

(2) *Sonographers*, also known as ultrasonographers, direct high frequency sound waves into areas of the body. The waves, collected by special equipment, come out as an image on a screen, a videotape or a photograph. The results are interpreted by radiologists, physicians who specialize in radiology.

Like radiographers, sonographers explain procedures to patients, position them, and program the equipment. Specialties within sonography include neurosonography (brain), vascular (blood flows), echocardiography (heart), abdominal (liver, kidneys, spleen, and pancreas), obstetrics and gynecology (female reproductive system), and ophthalmology (eye).

Other duties of radiologic technologists include maintaining patient records and diagnostic equipment. Some prepare work schedules and evaluate purchases of new equipment.

What it Takes to Succeed as a Radiologic Technologist

Radiologic equipment is delicate, and tests are expensive, so these professionals must be perfectionists about procedure. To obtain precise results, they must follow doctors' instructions exactly as explained. And to protect against any excessive exposure to radiation, they must adhere strictly to safety procedures.

Though radiologic technologists see many patients, they spend very little time with each one. As a result, people who thrive in this field prefer the scientific aspects of medicine.

The Inside Scoop on Radiologic Technology

Although doctors are often enthusiastic about the clinical benefits of new radiographic technologies, they don't always buy them as soon as they hit the market. The willingness of insurance companies to pay for new procedures drives many purchasing and hiring decisions. Ultrasound is becoming a popular alternative to radiologic procedures because it doesn't involve the hazards of radiation. This means sonographers will enjoy better job opportunities than radiographers. As employers look for ways to control their staffing costs, radiologic technologists trained and credentialed in more than one type of imaging technology will have better employment opportunities.

Career Ladder for Radiologic Technologists

- Department supervisor or manager (bachelor's or master's degree)
- Registered nurse
- Physician assistant
- Radiation therapist
- Respiratory therapist

Career Close-Ups

To Learn More

- For career information:

  American Society of Radiologic Technologists
  Phone: (505) 298-4500; (800) 444-2778
  Website: www.asrt.org
  Email: customerservices@asrt.org

  Society of Diagnostic Medical Sonographers
  Phone: (214) 473-8057; (800) 229-9506
  Website: www.sdms.org
  Email: info@sdms.org

  American Healthcare Radiology Administrators
  Phone: (978) 443-7591; (800) 334-AHRA
  Website: www.ahraonline.org
  Email: info@ahraonline.org

- For accredited radiology programs:

  Joint Review Committee on Education in Radiologic Technology
  Phone: (312) 704-5300
  Website: www.jrcert.org
  Email: mail@jrcert.org

- For a list of accredited diagnostic medical sonography programs:

  Commission on Accreditation of Allied Health Education Programs (CAAHEP)
  Website: www.caahep.org/programs/dms/dms-main.htm

10. Registered Nurse (R.N.)

Projected growth through 2008: 22 percent

Number of jobs by 2008: 2,530,000

Salary: $29,000 to $69,000 (Highest pay in temporary or personnel supply services, lowest in nursing and personal care facilities.)

Job Outlook

While hospitals will continue to need nurses, the fastest growth will be in home health, long term care, and ambulatory care (doctors' offices and clinics). As more complex medical procedures such as intravenous therapy (IV) are shifted to the home environment, home care nursing jobs will increase. The shift away from inpatient care will create new jobs in same-day surgery, emergency, chemotherapy, and rehab clinics. In nursing homes, R.N. jobs will increase 36 percent to meet the needs of the very elderly with Alzheimer's disease, strokes, and heart problems. 25 percent of RNs work part time, and 10 percent hold more than one job.

Practice Settings

- Hospitals: inpatient and outpatient departments (60 percent)
- Clinics, physicians' offices, home health care agencies, nursing homes, temporary help agencies, schools, and government agencies (35 percent)
- Residential care facilities, social service agencies, religious organizations, research facilities, business and public relations firms, insurance agencies, and private homes (5 percent)

Profile of an R.N.

Personality traits: Attentive to detail, compassionate, friendly, hard working, organized, self-confident, tactful

Skills: Anticipate the needs of others, communicate in a one-to-one setting, concentrate amid chaos, learn by reading, listen attentively, nurture people, observe behavior changes, organize tasks and schedules

Job setting: Different patients or clients each day, direct patient care, job security, large organization, work with adults, work with children

Career Close-Ups

Learning to be a Registered Nurse

There are three educational tracks in nursing, all of which qualify licensed graduates for entry-level positions as staff nurses. Two tracks, the A.D.N. and diploma, are described here. The third track, bachelor of science (B.S.N.) in nursing, is described in chapter 2, because of its long four- to five-year educational requirement. There are important differences in the responsibilities and advancement opportunities available to graduates with various nursing degrees.

Accredited programs: Over 2,200 in community colleges, four-year colleges and universities, and a few diploma programs in hospitals. About 50 percent of the programs offer A.D.N.s, and a small percentage offer diplomas in nursing.

Certification and credentials: All states require nurses to pass a national licensing exam. When they pass, they earn the R.N. credential. Many R.N.s indicate their educational background along with the R.N. For example, Jane Doe, R.N., A.D.N., or Donna Smith, R.N., B.S.N.

1. Associate Degree in Nursing (A.D.N.)

Length of training: Two years

While ADN graduates have no trouble finding jobs, the variety and responsibilities are somewhat limited, as are the advancement opportunities. Often, A.D.N. graduates accept hospital positions and work their way up to the B.S.N. level using tuition reimbursement from their employers.

2. Diploma in Nursing

Length of training: Two to three years

Like the A.D.N., a diploma in nursing provides a solid foundation for general patient care and further education.

Course work: All nursing programs cover basic anatomy, physiology, microbiology, chemistry, nutrition, psychology, behavioral sciences, and nursing practice. Bachelor's degree programs include more extensive nursing studies, liberal arts courses, and electives.

Field experience or externship: Hospitals, nursing homes, public health departments, home health agencies, and ambulatory clinics

Career Close-Ups

What Nursing is Really Like

RNs work in every aspect of health care: disease prevention; health education and research, and direct patient care. They assist physicians and develop care plans. An increasingly important role for nurses is to teach patients and their families how to handle complicated home care processes, whether it's taking care of surgical incisions or feeding a premature infant.

Hospital nurses provide bedside care and supervise L.P.N.s and aides. In this setting, most R.N.s specialize in one area, such as surgery or emergency care.

Office and clinic nurses prepare patients for exams, administer medications, treat wounds and incisions, and assist with surgery. They counsel patients in self-care for chronic problems like diabetes. At times they take on office duties and routine lab work.

Nursing home or long term care nurses manage the care of residents with conditions ranging from fractures to Alzheimer's disease. Instead of direct care, they usually develop care plans and supervise L.P.N.s and aides who work at the bedside. Occasionally, they start intravenous fluids or assess patients' conditions.

Home health nurses assess patients' home and family life and incorporate their findings into care plans for home health care visits. A good care plan for a terminal cancer patient living with his wife and three teenagers would not be right for a similar patient who is a bachelor living alone.

Public health nurses work in government and private agencies and clinics, schools, retirement communities, and other community settings. Primarily, they teach people about health, though they might also do immunizations, blood pressure screenings, and family planning instruction.

Occupational health or industrial nurses work in factories or offices. They provide emergency care or take care of minor illnesses. They might also prepare accident reports, counsel employees on physical fitness, or identify health/safety hazards.

What You Need to Succeed as an RN

Nurses need the diplomacy of an ambassador and the patience of a saint. They are usually responsible for implementing doctors' orders and coordinating the work of other care providers. They're often the go-betweens who interpret the doctors' orders to patients and families. As such, they must be able bear the brunt of the anger and frustration that often comes with illness.

Sometimes physicians can be rude, taking out their stress on nurses. Nurses might even find themselves in ethical binds when they disagree with a doctor's treatment plan or a family's decision on behalf of a patient.

The Inside Scoop on Registered Nursing

Hospital and nursing home jobs often involve night, weekend and holiday shifts. In facilities that are short-staffed, there is a good deal of overtime. Nurses with advanced training may be on call periodically. Hazards of the job include exposure to hepatitis, radiation, and in rare instances, to HIV or AIDS. Unfailing adherence to safety procedures is critical.

Nurses need the emotional stability to cope with human suffering and stress, says Jennifer Jacoby, R.N., M.S.N. "In hospitals they generally have to cope with a lot of hubbub. They need a high tolerance for multitasking. They have to enjoy being around people."

"A good nurse understands that the smallest things can make a difference, to their patients and to their coworkers. And it helps to admit when they don't know something or when they need help."

Jacoby adds that nursing can be hard physical labor. "It's not always pushing paper around on a desk," she says. It can also be emotionally exhausting, especially when dealing with patients suffering from abuse, violence, or serious physical deformities.

Career Ladder for Nurses
- Assistant head nurse and head nurse
- Health care management
- Nurse practitioner in a specialty such as geriatrics (elderly) or neonatology (newborns)
- Nursing Certificate in advanced specialties such as nurse-midwife (delivering babies) or anesthetist (putting patients to sleep or numbing parts of the body for surgery)

Career Close-Ups

To Learn More
- For nursing careers:

    National League for Nursing
    Phone: (212) 363-5555; (800) 669-1656
    Website: www.nln.org

    American Nurses Association
    Phone: (800) 274-4ANA
    Website: www.nursingworld.org

- For nursing education programs:

    American Association of Colleges of Nursing
    Phone: (202) 463-6930
    Website: www.aacn.nche.edu

11. Respiratory Therapist

Ranked #17 of 30 Hot Jobs
Projected growth through 2008: 43 percent
Number of jobs by 2008: 123,000
Salary: $26,000 to $47,000

Job Outlook

The best opportunities will be for therapists specializing in the care of extremely fragile newborns. In addition, respiratory therapists will be in high demand, prompted by three populatons: First, the elderly with heart and lung problems; second, accident victims, who now have better survival rates; and third, people requiring the temporary use of ventilators (breathing machines) for surgery and other treatments.

Practice Settings
- Hospitals (90 percent)
- Home health agencies, respiratory therapy clinics, and nursing homes (10 percent)

Career Close-Ups

Profile of a Respiratory Therapist

Personality traits: Accurate, analytical, attentive to detail, calm, compassionate, cooperative, dependable, efficient, patient, tolerant

Skills: Anticipate needs of others, concentrate amid chaos, learn by observing, listen attentively, nurture people, repair certain equipment, teach adults, teach children, work with technical data, work with numbers

Job setting: Different patients or clients each day, direct patient care, fast pace, flexible job description, job security, manual work with equipment, machines, etc., physical activity, work with adults, work with children

Learning to Be a Respiratory Therapist

Length of training: One year for a certificate; two years for an associate's degree; four years for a bachelor's degree

Course work: Anatomy and physiology, chemistry, physics, microbiology, math, therapeutic equipment and clinical tests

Field experience or externship: Mostly in hospitals and nursing homes

Accredited programs: Around 330 registered respiratory therapist programs and 135 certified respiratory therapist programs in hospitals, medical schools, colleges and universities, vocational schools, and the military.

Certification and credentials: The National Board for Respiratory Care offers voluntary certification and registration to graduates of accredited programs. Credentials awarded: Registered Respiratory Therapist (R.R.T.) or Certified Respiratory Therapist (C.R.T.). All graduates—from one-, two- or four-year programs—qualify to take the C.R.T. exam. C.R.T.s who meet educational and experience requirements qualify for the R.R.T. exam.

What Respiratory Therapy is Really Like

If you've ever had trouble breathing, then you can appreciate what respiratory therapy means to a person who *always* has trouble breathing. Respiratory therapists evaluate patients' lung capacity and analyze the oxygen, carbon dioxide, and hydrogen in their systems. By calculating a person's age, height, weight and gender, they determine the amount of deficiency in his breathing.

Career Close-Ups

Respiratory therapists work with asthmatics and people with lung diseases. They also work in emergency settings, treating stroke, heart attack and accident victims. The therapeutic equipment includes oxygen masks and nasal cannulas (nose tubes). Therapists also connect those unable to breathe to ventilators. They monitor the progress of all patients, adjusting oxygen flow and pressure as necessary.

Other therapeutic procedures include chest massage to stimulate coughing and removal of mucus from the lungs. They maintain respiratory equipment and teach patients how to prevent, or respond to breathing emergencies.

What it Takes to Succeed as a Respiratory Therapist

This occupation involves mathematical problem solving and the use of chemical and physical principles. For example, respiratory therapists compute medication dosages and calculate gas concentrations in the blood. Besides sensitivity to the human side of respiratory care, they need mechanical ability and manual dexterity to operate complicated equipment. Respiratory therapists have to be team players because they work in close conjunction with nurses, physicians, pharmacists, and other care givers.

The Inside Scoop on Respiratory Therapy

Most employers require applicants for entry-level or generalist positions to be CRTs or to be eligible for the exam. Supervisory positions and jobs in intensive care departments usually require the RRT (or RRT eligibility). Therapists are increasingly asked to expand their capabilities by learning to do electrocardiograms (EKG), stress testing and take blood samples. Employers offer on-the-job training for expanded duties.

Respiratory therapists work 35–40 hours a week, often on evening, night or weekend shifts. The job involves a great deal of standing and walking. The stress can run high when patients have emergencies.

Career Ladder for Respiratory Therapists
- Specialties within respiratory therapy, such as cardiopulmonary disorders
- Branch manager for home care and respiratory equipment rental firms
- Department manager
- Physician assistant
- Nurse clinician or nurse practitioner

Career Close-Ups

To Learn More

- For career information:

  American Association for Respiratory Care
  Phone: (972) 243-2272
  Website: www.aarc.org
  Email: info@aarc.org

- For respiratory therapy credentials:

  National Board for Respiratory Care, Inc.
  Phone: (913) 599-4200
  Website: www.nbrc.org
  Email: nbrc-info@nbrc.org

- For accredited educational programs:

  Committee on Accreditation for Respiratory Care
  Phone: (817) 283-2835
  Website: www.coarc.com

EARNINGS

Nonsupervisory workers in health care earn slightly higher annual salaries than those in all private industries. The houly earnings for nonsupervisory health care workers average $13.70, compared to $12.75 in all private industries. For example, dental assistants average $12.75 an hour, bus drivers $9.45 and hairdressers $9.10 an hour.

- Hospitals: $26,000
- Offices of physicians, dentists and other health practitioners: $20,400
- Home health services, nursing and personal care facilities: $15,700

In all service industries, including health care, the average annual earnings increased 6.8 percent between 1999 and 2000—from $31,500 to $33,670.

Segments of the health care industry with large numbers of part-time employees (home health, nursing, and personal care) show lower average annual earnings.

(Source: U.S. Bureau of Labor Statistics)

Career Close-Ups

OTHER HEALTH OCCUPATIONS NOT COVERED IN THIS BOOK

For details on the following occupations, check out the *Occupational Outlook Handbook* at your library or at www.bls.gov.

- Chiropractors
- Clinical laboratory technologists and technicians
- Dental laboratory technicians
- Dentists
- Dietitians and nutritionists
- Electroneurodiagnostic technologists
- Emergency medical technicians and paramedics
- Health services managers
- Medical secretaries
- Nuclear medicine technologists
- Nursing and psychiatric aides
- Ophthalmic laboratory technicians
- Opticians, dispensing
- Optometrists
- Pharmacists
- Physical therapists
- Physicians
- Podiatrists
- Psychologists
- Receptionists and information clerks
- Recreational therapists
- Social and human service assistants
- Social workers
- Speech-language pathologists and audiologists
- Veterinarians

PERSONAL PROFILE

John Hunyady
Certified Medical Assistant/Certified Phlebotomist

In 1998, John fulfilled a dream when he went to work in the outpatient department of a children's hospital. It took him 20-odd years to get there. After high school, he painted houses and owned a hot dog stand. "I did a little bit of everything," he says. "But I was always fascinated with how the human body works, and I wanted to get into health care." He finally did it after graduating from Maric College in San Diego. Today at age 44, he is certified in medical assisting and phlebotomy (drawing blood). "Helping people get through a disease or illness is the most rewarding career I could have chosen," he notes. "This is a job I like going to. I never look at my watch, wondering when my shift will be over."

What John Loves about His Work

For a guy who likes kids, you might wonder why he likes the job of drawing blood from their arms and fingers. He explains, "My emphasis is on talking with the kids. They're here because they're ill and my job is to make them feel comfortable." He talks them through procedures, explaining exactly what he's going to do and why. John's technique is so good that he's often called to draw blood from youngsters with fragile veins ravaged by long bouts of illness. "This work makes a difference in their lives and in their families' lives," he adds. His patients range from two days old to 10 years and older.

John's Biggest Challenge and How He Copes with It

"Sometimes the parents are a lot more difficult than the children," John observes. "They're so fearful for their kids' well-being that the kids pick up on it and get hysterical." That's when he pauses and gives the parents a little tender, loving care. Another challenge is children headed for heart surgery. "Some of them have been through such trauma and they die after all. But some of them heal!" he says. "And there's hope in most cases." For perspective, John keeps his eye on the big picture. "These lab tests have to be done prior to surgery. Without them, the kids would not get the right care."

For the moment, John wouldn't trade his position—even for a promotion. "I just had a chance to move up," he says. "But it would have meant no contact with patients and I turned it down."

How to Make the Most of Your Training

In the classroom, John advises, "pay attention to the subjects you don't really think will apply to your job." For example, he assumed the class on insurance coding was mainly for front office trainees, but in fact, he uses the training constantly, assigning billing codes to his lab tests.

When you get a job, attitude is everything, he says. "Suit up and show up! When you finish something, ask if there's anything else you can do. If you have that kind of attitude, you'll go places."

Chapter Four

PREPARING FOR YOUR CAREER

Now it's time to talk about training. Don't know where to start? Don't worry. You probably know a lot more than you realize and this chapter will help you fill in the gaps. By the time you finish, you'll be prepared to choose a school and apply for admission.

GROUNDWORK

First, pull together what you already know. Review your self-assessment results from the Introduction. That's your best guide for career decisions.

For each occupation you consider, ask whether it will enable you to function in a setting where you can do your best work. Do your personality traits suit the work? Would you get to use the skills you love? While it's rare to find a job that provides 100 percent of what you want, you probably won't last long if it provides too little. And if you took such a job, you wouldn't do your employer any favors, either.

- Take to heart the comments of health professionals throughout this book. While these folks love their work, they want to give newcomers a realistic picture of health care—it's a demanding field.
- As for education, do you want, or need, a fast track into your first health care position? If so, a certificate or associate's degree is ideal. If you can afford to spend more time and money up front so you can advance a little further early on, a bachelor's degree could be your best move.

At this point, do you know which occupation you want to pursue? If so, congratulations! Dig in and learn everything you can about it. If it's described in chapters 2 or 3, check out the resources in the Learn More section. If it's on the list of "Other Health Occupations Not Covered in this Book," check it out through the *Occupational Outlook Handbook* online or at your library. Also try a Web search using the occupation as your key word, or ask your local librarian to help. Contact the respective accrediting bodies to identify schools and training requirements. Many schools list the courses and testing requirements on their websites, and most will mail the information free of charge.

Perhaps you have a general idea of what you'd like, but haven't yet narrowed it down to one occupation. Maybe you'd prefer an outpatient setting to a hospital. Perhaps you'd like the business side better than direct patient care. That's a good start. Then, review chapters 2 and 3. If something sounds interesting on the list of "Other Health Occupations Not Covered in this Book," learn more through the *Occupational Outlook Handbook* or ask your librarian for help. Don't be shy about asking professional associations for job descriptions and lists of training programs. Members of the profession pay dues for this service; it's one of their recruitment tools. For local training resources, check your Yellow Pages under schools. When you call, ask to speak with the Admissions Department.

Still don't know exactly what you want to do? Remember that volunteer work can give you a hands-on view of what a field is really like. Job fairs are good places to gather bundles of ideas and information in a short period of time.

FINDING THE RIGHT TRAINING PROGRAM OR COLLEGE

Here are some guidelines for evaluating training institutions:
- Write down your questions and concerns. Have them with you when you visit or call.
- Visit the school with someone you trust—a parent, spouse, or friend. That way, you'll have another person with whom to compare notes.
- Does the admissions staff make time to talk with you? Do they answer your questions or get back to you when they find the answers?
- Is the program accredited? How long has it been in business?
- Review the curriculum. Have you met the prerequisites, if there are any?

- Does the application form suggest that the school is selective about its students? Michelle Groves describes her first visit to the San Antonio College of Medical and Dental Assistants: "I knew I was welcome. Still, I knew they were not going take me just because I walked into the admissions office. They were not hungry to take just anybody. I had to give them good reasons why I wanted to be a student."

In other words, beware of haphazard application procedures. They could be a clue that the institution is more interested in numbers than in selecting people who are likely to be a credit to their professions.

- Is financial aid available?
- What are the instructors' academic qualifications? How much practical experience do they have in the subject they teach?
- Compare the length of training and types of courses offered by different institutions. Programs leading to the same degree or certificate can vary as much as six months in length. Longer programs are likely to exceed the minimum training requirements and cost more. That's either an asset or a drawback, depending on your goals and resources.
- Is the school accessible? That might not seem like an issue now, but it could be a big one if you have an unreliable car or a young child to take to school each day.
- What's your overall impression? Do you feel welcome? Do the classrooms look like places where you'd be comfortable? Are the labs big enough and stocked with up-to-date equipment? Do the students appear interested and involved in what's going on? How about the teachers? Are they knowledgeable, friendly, confident, and receptive to questions?
- What is the student–teacher ratio? For lecture classes, 60:1 one might work. For labs and field training, 20:1 gives students the opportunity for individual attention.
- What are the job placement rates? "The program/school should be able to produce that information," advises Debbie Schroller, director of Career Services at the San Antonio College of Medical and Dental Assistants. "And you should be concerned if they don't produce it or if they don't give you straight answers!"

Preparing for Your Career

- Request the names, numbers or email addresses of recent graduates. Contact them and ask the questions on the "Discussion Points with Recent Grads" below. This input will be especially valuable if you're considering an out-of-town school.
- Find out whether credits from the core courses will transfer toward advanced training. This will be important when you make your next move up the career ladder.

TRAINING PROGRAM FACT SHEET

The sheet below will help you organize and compare findings from your school visits. Make photocopies of this page or put the information on the computer so you'll have one sheet for each facility you visit.

Date: _____

School or training program: _____
    Phone _____
    Address _____
    Website _____

Admissions director or contact person: _____
    Phone _____
    Fax _____
    Email _____

Department head: _____
    Phone _____
    Email _____

Career Services director: _____
    Phone _____
    Email _____

Job placement rates: _____

Tuition: _____
    Extra fees: Parking, lab supplies, etc. _____
    Books _____

Application deadline: _____

Application fee: _____

Length of training: _____

Prerequisites: _____

Certificate or degree awarded: _____

Size of classes: _____
    Student-to-teacher ratios (lectures/labs/field training) _____

Schedule: _____
    First day of class _____
    Class hours _____
    Graduation date _____

Recent graduates: _____
    1. Name _____
    Phone/Email _____
    2. Name _____
    Phone/Email _____

Overall impressions: _____
    Your impressions _____
    Your companion's impressions _____

Follow-up questions for staff: _____
    1. _____
    2. _____
    3. _____

Preparing for Your Career

DISCUSSION POINTS WITH RECENT GRADS

Name: _____

  Phone _____

  Email _____

Date of conversation: _____

  1. In general, did you get your money's worth from the training? _____
  _____

  2. Would you recommend the program to other students? _____
  _____

  3. How much time did you spend studying? Do you think that was more, less, or about the same as other students? _____
  _____

  4. Were the instructors helpful? _____
  _____

  5. Is it easy for students to get extra help if they need it? Is there an extra fee?
  _____

  6. What were the exams like?
  _____

  7. How much assistance did the Career Services department give with interviews and job placements? _____
  _____

  8. If you had it to do over again, would you sign up for the same certificate or degree? _____
  _____

  9. What is the school's reputation among employers? _____
  _____

  10. May I call you if I have more questions? _____
  _____

THE APPLICATION AND ADMISSION PROCESS

"The earlier you apply, the better. Some programs fill up fast," suggests John Hunyady. When he applied in October 1996, the first available opening was in January 1997. Many schools have various application dates each year. A few, like the Nebraska College of Business, accept applications all yearlong for all future enrollment dates.

If you have all your materials together, admission can be quick and painless. Nancie Froning, Director of Admissions at Maric College in San Diego, reports that most applicants receive answers within one week. Here are the basics:

- Evidence of high school graduation such as an official transcript bearing the graduation date, or an original diploma. Most of the time, a GED (General Education Development) certificate is acceptable.
- Completion of a skills test demonstrating minimum reading and writing abilities. The test is usually administered as part of the application.
- Informational interview with a representative of the school
- Tour of the school
- Complete financial arrangements, either by paying the tuition or submitting financial aid applications
- Health exam, tests, and immunizations prior to the externship or field training

MAKE THE MOST OF YOUR EDUCATION

If there was one common theme among what we heard from recent graduates, it was this: *Put your heart and soul into your training!* As Terrie Waters-Dunlap says, "This is not like high school where you have vacations. You'll study nights, weekends, and holidays. But hang in there: We need good people in this business!"

"Your studies have to come first," insists Loyda Morales. "If you take this attitude all through your program, then your certification exam will be easy."

Create Job Offers Beginning Your First Day of Class

When you realize that training institutions survive through the quality of their trainees, you'll understand that the better you manage yourself in the classroom, the better your job opportunities will be. If you show your commitment from day one, your instructors and the Career Service staff will be eager to match you up with the best employers.

Grades count, but there's more to it. Remember in chapter 2, what employers said about punctuality, attendance, and reliability? Your instructors will size you up against those standards as they confer with Career Services about externships and job possibilities. And it's those same instructors who will write your letters of recommendation.

Teresa Wiley explains how to demonstrate the qualities employers want. "Try to make every class. Each day you miss is knowledge you will miss. This is not like high school where you can blow off a day here or there. Your education determines how well you'll be able to do your job in the real world." If you *have* to miss a day, ask the teacher how you can catch up. If you have problems with a subject, arrange for extra help before you get in over your head.

"Some people get frustrated with all the work and information coming at them at once," says Loyda Morales. "But stick with it. Do the work 100 percent every day, in the classroom and during your externship—whether you're going to be hired after your externship or not." That philosophy served Loyda in an unexpected way.

As a student, she worked with a primary care physician, serving as a health fair volunteer. When it was over, they parted ways. Several months later however, he sought her out and asked her to work in his private practice as a medical assistant. That was nearly four years ago, and she's still there today.

Terrie Waters-Dunlap adds that volunteer service counts as experience on your resume. It's really more than work experience, adds Roland Cutting. "It shows a prospective employer something about where your heart is."

Visit Career Services Early and Often

The Career Services staff connect the school to the job market. They serve on committees and task forces in the community. They're always in touch with employers, scouting out externships and field training possibilities. This puts them on a first name basis with employers and gives them a first-hand view of developments in the job market. If a dentist needs a dental assistant or if a hospital needs a respiratory therapy assistant, the Career Services office is probably the first place they'll call. The staff follow students through their programs, tracking their grade point averages and giving them job leads. Many students have jobs in place even before they graduate.

"We urge students to get to know us and to visit us often," says Debbie Schroller. She adds that prospective students should make it a point to visit a school's Career

Services department. The department's role includes:
- Assistance with externships
- Posting information about career fairs
- Tips on "working" the career fairs
- Coaching in appropriate dress and professional conduct
- Teaching job search skills including resumes and interview techniques
- Writing letters of reference
- Finding and sharing job leads
- Follow-up throughout externships and first jobs to ensure a good fit for student and employer
- Lifetime career assistance

TO LEARN MORE

- *Directory of Private Career Schools and Colleges of Technology*, published by the Accrediting Commission of Career Schools and Colleges of Technology (ACCSCT), available in your high school guidance office or at your public library. Be sure to use the latest edition for the most current information.

You can also search ACCSCT's website by state, type of program, degree or certificate desired, or school name. For each school, the site posts degrees available, length of program and tuition.

Accrediting Commission of Career Schools and Colleges of Technology
Phone: (703) 247-4212
Website: www.accsct.org
Email: info@accsct.org

- The Yellow Pages are good for identifying local training programs. Check the listings for "Schools—Business and Vocational" or "Schools—Medical."

Preparing for Your Career

PERSONAL PROFILE

Terrie Waters-Dunlap
Licensed Vocational Nurse

Terrie worked in health care during the late 70s and early 80s, and then left the field until a life-changing experience reordered her priorities. "I decided to go back to what I always wanted—to be a nurse."

In 2001, after 18 months of hard work at the Maric College in San Diego, Terrie graduated as a licensed vocational nurse (L.V.N.). Today she works in a hospital and loves taking care of her elderly patients.

Reflections from a "Mature Student"

Terrie admits that going back to school at 42 was a shock to her system. She advises anybody who's considering a career college to go in with a clear understanding what's involved.

Believe it when the staff tell you it will take dedication to get through the program, she urges. "Talk with a recent graduate," she says, "Let them tell you about the absolute highs and lows, and the time you'll spend on your studies."

"Prepare to spend some of the longest nights of your life studying!" she suggests. "It can be frustrating, but in the end, it's well worth it. There are tons of jobs out there. When students come to me, I tell them, if I can do it, anybody can! I still don't know it all, she says, "but I'm learning more all the time."

In fact, the L.V.N. certificate is just the beginning for Terrie. She's seriously considering starting classes to become a registered nurse.

Chapter Five

PAYING FOR YOUR EDUCATION

The ideal way to pay for school is to write a check up front. But with current costs running anywhere from $2,000 to $100,000, few of us have the means. Before we get sidetracked on the high cost of getting an education, however, let's discuss the cost of *not* getting an education.

According to the latest U.S. Census Bureau figures, the median annual income for workers age 25 and over with:

- High school diploma is $27,150.
- College training, no degree is $32,200.
- Associate's degree is $35,100.
- Bachelor's degree is $44,000.

But the money is just one piece of it. You probably know this if you've ever talked with someone who's 40-something and still wishes he'd gone on to school. That regret is another cost of not getting an education.

Teresa Wiley, a registered medical assistant in New Braunfels, Texas contends, "These days, you even need some education to work at McDonald's, so why not find something you really love to do and get your training there? In health care, the work is rewarding financially and emotionally. And it's a secure field—you'll always have a job!"

PAY AS YOU GO OR GO FOR FINANCIAL AID?

One option is to work as you learn and graduate debt-free. That may be practical if:
- Your income is high enough to cover your living expenses and educational costs.
- You can arrange your schedule to manage classroom, homework, and personal obligations.

With night classes and a day job, or vice versa, some people do manage it. Loyda Morales worked part time during her training as a medical assistant, but she also received federal student loans. John Hunyady, on the other hand, opted for student loans with no outside job. "That way you can devote your full time and energy to furthering your career," he notes. "There's a small sacrifice to paying back the loans, but it's temporary and it will make a difference for the rest of your life."

It's a personal decision, says Elaine Neely-Eacona, Vice President of Financial Aid, at Quest Education Corporation in Atlanta, Georgia. She observes that the financial aid specialists at Quest encourage students to supplement their loan income during the classroom phase of their training, if they can maintain their grades. "But it's generally not possible to work during the externship," she adds.

Unless you can earn a handsome salary, it probably doesn't pay to postpone your education while you save for tuition, she suggests. "If you earn minimum wage, as most high-school graduates do, you're better off to start school and take out loans. After you have your certification, you'll earn two or three times minimum wage and you can pay back the loans in much less time than you could save in advance."

If financial aid seems a wise choice, the tools below will help you figure out how much to borrow.

ESTIMATE YOUR LIVING EXPENSES

One way to calculate your daily expenses is to record every single expenditure over three months. If you choose that method, it will mean carrying a pocket notebook and writing down every penny you spend and what it's spent for. Be sure to add in periodic expenses like auto insurance, license tags or registration fees, and repairs; health insurance and copays.

Another way to nail down your living expenses is to fill out a budget sheet such as the "Personal Expense Estimates" below. This picture of your spending habits might help you tighten the budget you have planned for school. For example, could you pack your lunch instead of visiting the vending machine? Could you tape programs on TV instead of renting movies? The blunt truth is, your "entertainment" might come down to an extra hour of sleep, especially in a career training program!

PERSONAL EXPENSE ESTIMATES

Skipping the items that don't apply to you, sort the "yearly expenses" column into what you'll have to spend during training. Those numbers will plug into your estimated educational expense table.

Expense	1st month	2nd month	3rd month	Yearly
Housing				
Rent or house payment				
Electricity				
Heat & air conditioning				
Water bill				
Trash pick-up				
Phone and long distance				
Internet connection				
Cable service				
Transportation*				
Car payment				
Auto insurance				
License or registration fee				
Repairs				
Gas				
Bus fare				
Parking				
Food				
Groceries				
Restaurant meals & snacks				

Paying for Your Education

Health insurance				
Monthly premiums				
Co-pays				
Prescriptions & over-the-counter drugs				
Other insurance				
Renter's				
Life				
Other				
Dependent care				
Child care				
Child support				
Alimony				
Other				
Credit card payment				
Clothing				
Self				
Dependent(s)				
Personal care services & products				
Self				
Dependent(s)				
Entertainment				
Other expenses				
1.				
2.				
3.				

* If you move away for training, your transportation costs may include occasional visits back home.

If you'd rather computerize your expense records, try one of the personal finance packages from a software store for around $25, or go to www.personalbudgeting.com for a sample budget.

Paying for Your Education

ESTIMATE YOUR INCOME

Fill in the amounts you expect to receive while you are in school.

Expected Income	Monthly	Yearly
Personal earnings (take home)		
Savings or investment income		
Family contribution (spouse, parents, grandparents, etc.)		
Child support		
Alimony		
Aid to Families with Dependent Children (AFDC)		
Veterans benefits		
Social Security		

ESTIMATE YOUR EDUCATIONAL EXPENSES

You'll hear the term *Cost of Attendance* in connection with student loans. Here's the definition: The estimated total amount it will cost to go to school. It's usually expressed as a yearly figure.

Cost of Attendance	
Tuition and fees	
Room and board (on-campus costs or allowance for off-campus residence)	
Books	
Supplies	
Transportation	
Loan fees	
Care of a dependent	
Costs related to a disability, such as a special wheelchair to get around campus or tutoring beyond the school's normal offering	
Miscellaneous expenses such as rental or purchase of a computer	
Reasonable costs connected with employment in a cooperative education program (the cost of a uniform, for example).	

HOW MUCH FINANCIAL AID WILL YOU NEED?

If your expected income is less than your cost of living and educational expenses, financial aid is your best alternative.

The amount of student financial aid (SFA) for which you may qualify is based on the U.S. Department of Education's *financial need* formula:

    Cost of Attendance
    − <u>Expected family contribution</u> (from you and your family)
    = Financial need

The financial aid administrator at the school will put together a financial aid package that comes as close as possible to your need. But federal funds are limited, so you may receive less than your official "financial need."

Student Financial Aid (SFA): Thumbnail Sketch

There are three types of financial assistance. While the majority of accredited technical schools and colleges offer financial aid, they don't necessarily have all the programs.

A *grant* is money that does not have to be repaid. The amount of a grant is based on need, training costs and enrollment status—even less than half-time enrollment.

- Pell Grants recently ranged from $400 to $3,300 per school year.
- Federal Supplemental Educational Opportunity Grants ranged from $100 to $4,000.

A *loan* is money that must be repaid with interest. Loans are made to students or parents paying for a child's schooling.

- Direct Loan Program from the federal government
- Federal Family Education Loan Program through private lenders
- Perkins Loans offered by some schools to the neediest students
- Federal PLUS Loans are made to qualifying parents of dependent students

Work-study is money for education paid by the school for on-campus or community-based work.

Paying for Your Education

Who Gets SFA?

To be eligible for financial aid, you must:

- Be a U.S. citizen or eligible noncitizen of the United States with a valid social security number
- Have a high school diploma, General Education Development (GED) certificate, or pass a federally approved "ability to benefit" test
- Enroll in an eligible program as a regular degree or certificate student
- Register (or have registered) for selective service (the military), if you are a male between ages 18 and 25

How Do You Get SFA?

Application for federal student assistance is free. Some institutions do charge an application fee for institutional grants or scholarships.

1. Complete the Free Application for Federal Student Aid (FAFSA). Start early—as soon as you decide to apply to a training program. In fact, many technical or career schools will help you apply. Copies of the form are also available through your high school guidance office, college, or career school financial aid office, public libraries, the Federal Student Aid Information Center (800) 433-3243, or www.fafsa.ed.gov.

For most assistance, you need only the FAFSA or FAFSA renewal. If your parents apply for a loan, they'll have to complete additional forms. A FAFSA renewal is usually enough for the second year you apply for SFA. It's basically an update of any changes that have taken place since you filed the original FAFSA.

2. If you submit the FAFSA *on your own*, you'll receive a Student Aid Report (SAR) within one to four weeks, listing your Expected Family Contribution (the amount you and your family are expected to contribute toward your education). That amount may not match what you and your family end up contributing. If you submit the FAFSA *through the school*, they will tell you how much aid they can offer.

Paying for Your Education

> **FINANCIAL AID APPLICATION CHECKLIST**
>
> Before you sit down to complete the FAFSA, gather up the necessary paperwork. Actually, says Elaine Neely-Eacona of Quest Education, "filling out an application is much like filing an income tax return." At career and technical schools, "students typically start classes in January, so use that year's tax return even if you haven't filed it yet," she suggests. (For a January 2003 enrollment, use your 2002 tax return.)
>
> - Driver's license
> - Social Security card
> - W-2 Forms (Tax documents from employers stating wages paid during the year) and records of other earnings from the previous year
> - Previous year's income tax return (IRS Form 1040, 1040A, 1040EZ, Trust Territory tax return, or foreign country tax return)
> - Records of untaxed income, such as welfare, Social Security, Aid to Families with Dependent Children (AFDC) or Aid to Dependent Children (ADC), Temporary Assistance to Needy Families (TANF) or veterans benefits
> - Current bank statements
> - Current mortgage information for businesses and investments
> - Business and farm records
> - Records of stocks, bonds, and other investments
>
> Keep these records! If you file a paper FAFSA, do not mail documents from the above list with your form.
>
> (For more information on completing the FAFSA, go to www.fafsa.ed.gov and click on *Filling Out a FAFSA*.)

SFA Close-Ups

1. FEDERAL PELL GRANT

This is money that does not have to be repaid.

Points of Interest:

- School disburses the funds.
- Amounts are based on full time or half time enrollment status.
- Students receive only one Pell Grant in a school year.
- The Department of Education guarantees participating schools enough money to award Federal Pell Grants to its eligible students.

Who Qualifies?

The Department of Education uses a standard formula based on the student's Expected Family Contribution.

How Much Money Could a Student Receive?

The allocation varies with the federal budget. Recently, the maximum was $3,300. The award for individual students is calculated on the Expected Family Contribution and the Cost of Attendance.

How Is the Money Distributed?

The school can credit the Pell Grant to your school account, pay you directly, or both. Schools must notify students how, when, and how much they will be paid. It's at least once each term.

2. FEDERAL SUPPLEMENTAL EDUCATIONAL OPPORTUNITY GRANT (FSEOG)

This is money that does not have to be repaid. It goes to students with exceptional financial need.

Points of Interest:
- There is no guarantee that schools will receive FSEOGs for all eligible students.
- Students who receive Federal Pell Grants are given highest priority.

Who Qualifies?

Students with the lowest Expected Family Contributions.

How Much Money Could a Student Receive?

The amount varies between $100 and $4,000 a year, depending on when the student applies, the level of need, funds available, and the school's financial aid policies.

How Is the Money Distributed?

A school may credit the student's account or pay directly. Payments are made at least once per term.

Paying for Your Education

The following three loans, Stafford, PLUS, and Consolidation Loans, are available through two programs: Direct Loan Program (money loaned by the federal government), and Federal Family Education Loan Program (money loaned by private financial institutions such as banks and credit unions). Schools tends to use one or the other program; the major difference is the source of funds. Loan repayment options vary slightly.

Some student loans are partially subsidized. This means the Department of Education pays interest while the student is in school, and during grace and deferment periods. Unsubsidized loans incur interest for the life of the loan.

3. STAFFORD LOANS

This type of loan is the major educational self-help program.

Points of Interest:

- A one-time loan fee of up to 4 percent is deducted from the money received by the borrower.
- Interest rates vary annually, depending on prevailing interest rates, but they never exceed 8.5 percent.

Who Qualifies?

Half-time and full-time students in eligible programs.

How Much Money Could a Student Borrow?

Dependent students may borrow up to $2,625 the first academic year. After completing the first academic year, they may borrow up to $3,500 for the second full academic year. They may then borrow up to $5,500 for each full academic year.

Independent students (and dependent students whose parents are not eligible for Federal PLUS Loans) may borrow up to $6,625 the first academic year, and $7,500 for the second full academic year. They may then borrow up to $10,500 for each full academic year.

How Is the Money Distributed?

The school receives the funds, and pays at least two installments. It goes first to tuition and fees, and if applicable, room and board. The student gets the rest.

4. PLUS LOANS

This is money loaned to parents with good credit histories to pay for a dependent child's educational expenses.

Points of Interest:

- If parents are unable to pass a credit check, they may still be able to receive a PLUS Loan if a relative or friend can pass the credit check and agree to pay in the case that the parents are unable.
- In some instances, parents may pass a credit check if they show legitimate reasons for a poor credit history.
- Parents start the application process by contacting the school's financial aid office.
- Since the PLUS Loan is not based on need, completion of a FAFSA may not be required. School policies vary.
- Interest rates vary annually, depending on prevailing interest rates, but never exceed 9 percent.
- A 4 percent loan fee is deducted proportionately from each payment.

Who Qualifies?

Parents who meet citizenship requirements as explained in "Who Gets SFA?" earlier in this chapter. They must also be current with payment of other SFA loans in their names.

How Much Could Parents Borrow?

The annual limit is equal to the Cost of Attendance minus any other financial aid the student receives.

How Is the Money Distributed?

The lender sends the money to the school. It is usually paid out in two installments. The funds go first to tuition, fees, other school charges, and room and board if applicable. Any remaining money goes directly to the parents unless they authorize release to the student or to the student's school account.

5. CONSOLIDATION LOAN

This is a repayment option enabling the borrower to combine several types of federal student loans into one loan with one monthly payment. Even a single loan can be rolled into a Consolidation Loan to take advantage of the flexible repayment options.

Points of Interest:
- Sometimes the interest on a Consolidation Loan is lower than the original loan. Interest rates vary, but never exceed 8.25 percent.
- No money is distributed in Consolidation Loans. They simply enable the borrower to scale down the number of monthly payments.

Who Qualifies?
Most borrowers may apply for Consolidation Loans. They may apply while still in school or during the repayment period. Schools distribute information about Consolidation Loans during entrance and exit counseling sessions.

6. FEDERAL PERKINS LOAN

This is a low-interest (5 percent) loan. Perkins Loans are not connected with the Direct or Federal Family Education Loan programs.

Points of Interest:
- Perkins Loans are made from government funds and a share contributed by the school.
- The school is considered the lender on a Perkins Loan.
- Perkins Loans are repaid to the school.
- There are no loan fees.

Who Qualifies?
The neediest students.

How Much Could a Borrower Receive?
Depending on the level of need, as well as funds available from the school, a student may borrow up to $4,000 a year.

How Is the Money Distributed?
The school usually pays the student directly or credits the school account. Generally, at least two payments are made during the academic year.

Paying for Your Education

7. FEDERAL WORK–STUDY

This program involves jobs to help students pay their educational expenses

Points of Interest:
- The program encourages community service work and work related to a student's course of study.
- Jobs are both on and off campus. Campus jobs usually involve working for the school.
- Off-campus work-study jobs must be in nonprofit organizations or public agencies. The work must be in the public interest.

Who Qualifies?

Students with "financial need" as defined by the Department of Education's SFA formulas. The timing of the student's application and available funds determine who receives work-study assistance.

How Much Money Could a Student Earn?

Wages are equal to, or higher than, the federal minimum wage, depending on the type of job and skills required. The amount a student earns may not exceed his total Federal work-study award. When assigning work hours, the employer or financial aid administrator will consider the student's class schedule and academic progress.

How Is the Paycheck Distributed?

The school must pay students directly at least once a month. A student may request deposits to a bank account or application toward school expenses.

Repayment

Most of these loans have similar repayment guidelines. You'll receive the details when you sign the paperwork to initiate the loan. Here are a few highlights.

Student loan repayment plans are generally as follows:

Standard: Fixed amount, at least $50 a month, up to 10 years
Extended: At least $50 a month, spread over 12 to 30 years

Graduated: Lower payments immediately after school increasing over 12 to 30 years
Income contingent: Monthly payments based on income, family size and loan amount

Before the first payment comes due, you have a six-month grace period. It starts when you graduate, leave school, or drop below half-time enrollment. It's longer than six months if you are on active duty with the military.

PLUS Loans have no grace period. Parents must begin repayment within 60 days after the final loan disbursement for each school term. This means that parents start paying while the student is still in school. The maximum repayment period is 10 years.

Permission to postpone or reduce payments beyond the grace period takes two forms:

(1) *Deferment* is granted for half- or full-time enrollment in school, inability to find full-time employment, economic hardship, or certain types of public service or employment. Medical Assistant Loyda Morales for instance, has a deferment because she is enrolled half-time in classes for her nursing degree. Nonetheless, she says, "Whenever I get a little extra money, I put it toward the interest on my loans. Although I don't have to, it will help later when I start making payments again."

Loans may be deferred or fully forgiven for graduates who work full time as nurses or medical technicians. Loans are partially forgiven for graduates volunteering in Vista or the Peace Corps.

(2) *Forbearance* is granted in periods of poor health or personal problems, and for certain types of employment. During these periods, interest varies according to the reason for postponement and nature of the loan.

A loan may be fully forgiven if the borrower dies or becomes totally and permanently disabled. And a loan may be partially or fully forgiven if the school closes before the student can complete the program of study, if the school submits a false loan certification, or if the school fails to return the loan funds to the lender.

An Unpaid Creditor Is an Ugly Thing!

When you graduate and those first paychecks roll in, the temptation to spend will seem unbearable. And the grace period will fly by. The monthly loan payments will come due. And you'll have some serious responsibility on your hands.

Financial aid lenders take harsh action when borrowers default (fail to make payments). They notify national credit bureaus, which wrecks your credit rating for a long time. That makes it tough to borrow money for a car or house. Lenders may also deduct payments and collection expenses from your paycheck. The Department of Education could authorize the Internal Revenue Service to deduct the overdue payments from your income tax refunds. Defaulting endangers your chances of receiving more federal financial aid.

Even if you happen not to receive a bill or repayment notice, you're still responsible for paying the set amount. The lender will probably send notices or coupon books in advance, but it's a good idea to watch for them two months before your grace period ends. If nothing arrives, say, six weeks prior to your first payment date, call to be sure everything is in order. Make sure to keep copies of all your loan documents.

If you apply for deferment or forbearance, you're responsible for payments until the lender confirms that your request has been granted. You're responsible for notifying the loan representative if you drop below half-time enrollment, or change your name, address, or Social Security Number.

"Free Money"

"Financial aid needs to be carefully explored. Make sure you have enough money for school, and find as much free money as you can," advises Terrie Waters-Dunlap. "I got a lot of loans. But now I know there are a lot of grants I didn't know about before I made the loans. And the more free money you get, the less you'll have to repay in the end," she explains.

Scholarships and grants are not just for the academic elite. For sure, some are geared toward academic achievement. But others are based on gender, financial need, field of study, ethnicity, or place of residence—or as incentives to work in a geographic location or line of work. Two- and four-year colleges offer some scholarships and grants. Of course, the tradeoff is the higher cost of attendance than career or technical schools.

We're not going to tell you that free money is easy to come by. You'll have to hustle and sift out the programs for which you qualify. Yes, there are search firms that claim they'll do it for you. "We discourage that," cautions Elaine Neely-Eacona. "We've never seen an instance of anyone receiving a significant amount of money through national search firms. We tell students to do their own footwork."

Where Do I Start?

A good way to acquaint yourself with the subject is to spend an hour or so browsing through a CD-ROM or a directory of scholarships and grants. If you're in high school, check the resources in the counseling office.

Here's a list of leads for starters. As soon as you get the hang of it, you can delete and add sources specific to your goals.

- State department of education
- City job services agency
- County health department
- Professional societies and associations. If you're considering one of the occupations in chapters 2 or 3, be sure to contact the professional organizations listed after each occupational description.
- Health care organizations, e.g., Diabetes Association or American Heart Association
- Hospitals
- Businesses (Some businesses give educational awards to children of employees)
- Labor unions
- Civic groups and fraternal organizations, e.g., American Legion, 4-H Clubs, Girl Scouts, Boy Scouts
- Charitable and educational foundations
- Religious organizations
- State associations of career educators or career education institutions

Search Aids

- Key words to find local groups through the Yellow Pages: associations, clubs, organizations
- Key words for online searches: scholarships, grants, health care, and your field of interest, like occupational therapy
- Key words to locate professional associations or societies representing an occupation: associations, society, academy, plus the field, e.g., health care administration

PERSONAL PROFILE

Teresa Wiley
Registered Medical Assistant

Teresa got her first exposure to health care right after high school when she took a course in emergency medical technology. Ten years later, in 2000, she launched her career as a registered medical assistant.

"There are so many possibilities for advancement in this job and it's a field that will always be needed," she says. "I wish somebody had told me to do this right out of high school," says the 29-year-old mother of three. She views her present job in a cardiology office as the first rung on her career ladder.

What Teresa Loves about Her Work

"I love the people and helping them understand what their bodies are doing," she says. "It's rewarding to teach them about the medical techniques that keep us alive so much longer. Trying to absorb all that knowledge and relay it to my patients is a huge challenge," Teresa notes.

She researches each new technique as it's adopted by her employer and asks volumes of questions. From time to time, she pulls out the text books from her medical assisting classes at the San Antonio College of Medical and Dental Assistants in San Antonio, Texas. "In this work, we have to take our jobs seriously because we're dealing with people's lives."

Where Teresa Plans to Go from Here

"I plan to 'crawl' up the ladder," she quips. Her next step will be a licensed vocational nursing certificate, followed by a nursing degree. "You get more respect from the physicians and nurses when you start from the bottom of the ladder," she says. In the long term, she plans to become an emergency room nurse and will take paramedic's training along the way.

A Suggestion from Someone Who's Been There

If you plan to go to school, Teresa advises, "put your whole heart into it! Get serious. Ask a lot of questions. Get to know your counselors and department heads. And do your best work."

FINANCIAL AID RESOURCES

- The Student Guide: Financial Aid is the best federal financial aid overview. It details all the programs discussed in this chapter. It lists websites and phone numbers to related federal and state organizations. Download it or request a free copy from:

Federal Student Aid Information Center
P.O. Box 84
Washington, DC 20044-0084
Phone: (800) 433-3243
Website: www.ed.gov/studentaid

The website also links you to the Department of Education's vast financial aid services and resources.

- FAFSA (Free Application for Federal Student Aid) assistance provides online and print FAFSA forms. Free copies of the forms are also available from libraries as well as the Federal Student Aid Information Center, above.
Phone: (800) 801-0576

> **HINTS: MONEY RESOURCES**
> - Check your library's reference department for these and other free money directories.
> - Always use the latest editions.
> - If the source is over a year old, verify the contact information before you submit an application.

- The federal government's huge student website has links to government resources for planning and paying for your education. You can use the site to search for a job, access other government services, and even to file your taxes.
Phone: (800) USA-LEARN
Website: www.students.gov
Email: usa_learn@ed.gov

- *Scholarships 2003* (Kaplan, Inc., Simon & Schuster, New York, 2002). This directory features indexes to locate awards for students at various educational levels and fields of study.

- *Directory of Financial Aids for Women 2001–2003:* A Listing of Scholarships, Fellowships, Loans, Grants, Awards and Internships by Gail Ann Schlachter (Reference Service Press, El Dorado Hills, CA, 2001). Assistance is arranged by categories such as scholarships, loans, etc. Programs are also indexed by sponsoring organizations, geographic region in which assistance is granted and subject area. The directory describes 559 programs by application deadline, duration and amount of the award, and eligibility. It lists other directories of assistance for women including books and websites.

- *2000-2002 High School Senior's Guide to Merit and Other No-Need Funding,* by Gail Ann Schlachter and R. David Weber (Reference Service Press, 2000). The guide includes state sources of financial aid and grants as well as contests and other awards. Descriptions include the guidelines and deadlines for application. The book also lists websites for additional sources of free money.

- The Health Resources and Services Administration supports 40 programs that award 1,400 grants each year to health training programs. The emphasis is on diversity in the health care workforce. Grants help prepare professionals to serve diverse populations and underserved communities. To learn more, contact:
  HRSA Grants Application Center
  Phone: (877) 477-2123
  Website: www.hrsa.gov/grants.htm
  Email: hrsagac@hrsa.gov

- FinAid is a one-stop website for financial aid. It's a free resource for all users. Users may sign up for personalized scholarship leads by keying in data about their educational goals and information related to eligibility for awards. The site explains student loans and offers calculators to figure college costs, financial aid loan payments, and other school-related financial matters.
  Website: www.FinAid.org

- For details about service positions that lead to deferment or partial forgiveness of educational loans, contact the Peace Corps or Vista Volunteers.
  Peace Corps
  Paul D. Coverdell Peace Corps Headquarters
  111 20th St. NW
  Washington, DC 20526
  Phone: (800) 424-8580
  Website: www.peacecorps.gov/contact

  Vista Volunteers
  Website: www.americorps.org
  Email: Questions@americorps.org

Chapter Six

MOVING AHEAD

By now you know that health care and health careers change constantly. If you go into the field, you'll find your work life evolving for several reasons:

1. You will update your techniques to keep up with new discoveries in health care technology.

Here are two of many examples:

- Health information technology changes as medicine changes. New procedures mean that health information technicians must learn new codes for recording information on patient records and insurance claims.

    In fact, the growing volume of health information spurred the creation of a Certified Coding Specialist (CCS) credential. Procedures are so specialized that there's a separate credential for health information workers in physicians' offices: Certified Coding Specialist—Physician-based (CCS-P).

- Radiologic technologists can broaden their job opportunities by expanding their skills beyond standard X-ray techniques. They can learn to operate newer technologies like computerized tomography scanners (CT scanners) and magnetic resonance imaging (MRI) machines.

2. You seek new challenges after mastering one area.

If you start as a personal care assistant, you might find in a couple years that you're ready move on to licensed practical nursing or perhaps medical assisting. If you start as a dental assistant, you might become a dental hygienist. And if you're anything like Loyda Morales in chapter 1, your first training experience will awaken a zesty appetite for learning that takes you back to the classroom right away.

3. You look for more job security, more interesting work, better pay, or greater decision-making responsibilities.

Roland Cutting went on to earn a Bachelor of Business Administration after completing his military service, thus qualifying himself for administrative jobs.

4. You discover that your calling is toward a specialized niche in your field.

As we saw in earlier chapters, people shape their careers in different ways. Jennifer Jacoby took a package of expertise in nursing, married it to other skills, and changed her direction. She moved from direct patient care to management of nursing care for a hospital.

Carol Ellstrom trained as a nurse and discovered that she loves the educational side of nursing. So she coupled her nursing degree with a master's in adult and continuing education. Today she heads a hospital staff education department.

Kristin Gargano worked as a respiratory therapist and eventually took a job as medical assisting instructor and department head at a technical college.

John Hunyady earned his medical assisting certificate and expanded his skills with a phlebotomy certificate. Currently he works in the lab at a children's hospital. But if he ever had the need or desire, he could step into a back-office medical assisting role.

5. You find a better match for your skills in a different health care occupation.
- Ambulance drivers often become nurses, physician assistants or highly skilled emergency medical technicians.
- A hospital or retail pharmacy technician might join a drug manufacturing company as a sales representative.

6. You move into a newly created health occupation.

Some health occupations that will emerge during your work life don't even have a name yet because the discoveries that will support them are still in the research stage. A recent example is radial keratotomy (RK) or Lasik surgery, the laser eye surgery to correct nearsightedness. This procedure has created a new ophthalmology specialty, separate from the fitting of eyeglasses and contact lenses.

Other discoveries are underway, even as you read this. Perhaps one of them will change your health occupation. Actually, the rate of change could make you dizzy at times. Unsettling as it may be, though, nothing will change so much that you have to start over.

The Unchanging Core of Your Career

Have you noticed how we used terms like *expanded*, *layered on*, and *married* in describing career changes? Those words suggest adding on to something that's already in place. And that's exactly what happens—some things stay with you.

No matter how far your career path might take you from your original training and job description, you'll always have that core of inborn skills, traits, and job preferences you identified through the self-assessment tools in the Introduction. If the prospect of an ever-changing work scene shakes you up a bit, you can find security by counting those assets. On the other hand, you may find some exciting challenges when you want to strengthen or tone down any of those skills or traits. Consider those your growth opportunities. You'll find huge satisfaction in your progress.

The knowledge you acquire from your training is another piece of stability. Think of it: Almost every health care certificate or degree program requires that you learn human anatomy, the organs, muscle groups, and bones. You won't have to relearn them when you go for further training. They won't change!

If your career ladder takes you up the ranks of one profession, each new credential or degree will build on the previous one. In nursing, for instance, your knowledge from the associate's degree is the foundation for your bachelor of science in nursing (B.S.N.).

Even if your career path doesn't follow a straight vertical line, your existing knowledge and experience will still serve you. Your communication skills with patients and coworkers will never be out of date. Neither will the work habits that mark you as a star employee.

EACH CAREER TAKES ITS OWN SHAPE

A vertical path is one alternative, with a series of jobs progressing up the ladder in one occupation. A certified pharmacy technician might become a pharmacist, for instance, and eventually become manager of a hospital or retail pharmacy.

An alternate path might be made up of lateral moves—similar job responsibilities in different settings. A pharmacist or a pharmacy technician might go from the hospital pharmacy into pharmaceutical research, for example.

Sometimes, people switch occupations altogether. An occupational therapy assistant might become a physical therapist, for instance. Whatever shape your career takes, you can expect training and retraining as a fact of life. There will be seminars and workshops sponsored by your employer, certificates earned through night classes, weekend courses, and even time out from full-time work as you push toward a new educational goal.

When you need to discuss career decisions after graduation, remember that reputable technical schools offer their graduates lifetime career assistance. Also keep in mind that financial aid programs offer a built-in benefit for career advancement: You can postpone loan payments whenever you enroll as a half-time or full-time student.

All of this means that you can count on four things if you choose a health career.

1. You will not get bored.
2. Your work will always be a service to others.
3. There will always be plenty of jobs.
4. There will be endless opportunities to develop and advance.

Kaplan Higher Education

Kaplan Higher Education,
the higher education division of Kaplan, Inc.
(www.questeducation.com), is a leading education and
career training provider that offers diversified, career-oriented,
postsecondary education to more than 18,000 students at
45 campuses located in 13 states.

Kaplan Higher Education offers a variety of bachelor degree,
associate degree, and diploma/certificate programs in fields such as
health care, information technology, business, legal studies,
electronics, design and graphic arts, and various vocational trades.
Its curricula include programs leading to entry-level employment
in ten of the fifteen fastest growing occupations
(measured by percentage growth from 1994 through 2005)
as projected by the U.S. Department of Labor.

Kaplan Higher Education

ARIZONA

Long Technical College
13450 N. Black Canyon Hwy.
Suite 104
Phoenix, AZ 85029
(602) 548-1955

Phoenix Career College
First American Title Bldg.
111 W. Monroe Avenue, Suite 800
Phoenix, AZ 85003
(602) 252-2171

CALIFORNIA

Andon College
1700 McHenry Village Way, Suite 5
Modesto, CA 95350
(209) 571-8777

Andon College
1201 N. El Dorado Street
Stockton, CA 95202
(209) 462-8777

California College of Technology
4330 Watt Avenue, Suite 400
Sacramento, CA 95660
(916) 649-8168

Maric College
3666 Kearney Villa Road, Suite 100
San Diego, CA 92123
(858) 279-4500

Maric College
2030 University Drive
Vista, CA 92083
(760) 630-1555

Modern Technology College
6180 Laurel Canyon Blvd., Suite 101
North Hollywood, CA 91606
(818) 763-2563

COLORADO

Denver Career College
8 South Nevada Avenue, Suite 101
Colorado Springs, CO 80903
(719) 444-0190

Denver Career College
1401 19th Street
Denver, CO 80202
(303) 295-0550

IOWA

Hamilton College
2302 West First Street
Cedar Falls, IA 50613
(319) 277-0220

Hamilton College
3165 Edgewood Parkway, SW
Cedar Rapids, IA 52404
(319) 363-0481

Hamilton College
4655 121st Street
Des Moines, IA 50323
(515) 727-2100

Hamilton College
100 First Street, NW
Mason City, IA 50401
(641) 423-2530

Kaplan College
1801 E. Kimberly Road, Suite 1
Davenport, IA 52807
(563) 355-3500

MARYLAND

Hagerstown Business College
18618 Crestwood Drive
Hagerstown, MD 21742
(301) 739-2670

TESST College of Technology
1520 South Caton Avenue
Baltimore, MD 21227
(410) 644-6400

TESST College of Technology
4600 Powder Mill Road
Beltsville, MD 20705
(301) 937-8448

TESST College of Technology
803 Glen Eagles Court
Towson, MD 21286
(410) 296-5350

NEBRASKA

Bauder College
Phipps Plaza
3500 Peachtree Road, NE
Atlanta, GA 30326
(404) 237-7573

Lincoln School of Commerce
1821 K Street
Lincoln, NE 68508
(402) 474-5315

Nebraska College of Business
3350 North 90th Street
Omaha, NE 68134
(402) 572-8500

NEW HAMPSHIRE

Hesser College
25 Hall Street, Suite 104
Concord, NH 03301
(603) 225-9200

Hesser College
3 Sundial Avenue
Manchester, NH 03103
(603) 668-6660

Hesser College
410 Amherst Street
Nashua, NH 03063
(603) 883-0404

Hesser College
170 Commerce Way
Portsmouth, NH 03801
(603) 436-5300

Hesser College
1A Keewaydin Drive
Salem, NH 03079
(603) 898-3480

Kaplan Higher Education

OHIO

Ohio Institute of Photography and Technology
2029 Edgefield Road
Dayton, OH 45439
(937) 294-6155

Technology Education College
288 S. Hamilton Road
Columbus, OH 43213
(614) 759-7700

PENNSYLVANIA

CHI Institute
Lawrence Park Shopping Center
1991 Sproul Road, Suite 42
Broomall, PA 19008-3516
(610) 353-7630

CHI Institute
520 Street Road
Southampton, PA 18966
(215) 357-5100

ICM School of Business and Medical Careers
10 Wood Street
Pittsburgh, PA 15222
(412) 261-2647

Thompson Institute
2593 Philadelphia Avenue
Chambersburg, PA 17201
(717) 709-9400

Thompson Institute
5650 Derry Street
Harrisburg, PA 17201
(717) 564-4112

Thompson Institute
3440 Market Street
Philadelphia, PA 19104
(215) 387-1530

TENNESSEE

Southeastern Career College
2416 21st Avenue South, Suite 300
Nashville, TN 37212
(615) 269-9900

TEXAS

Career Centers of Texas—El Paso
8360 Burnham Road, Suite 100
El Paso, TX 79907
(915) 595-1935

San Antonio College of Medical and Dental Assistants
3900 North 23rd Street
McAllen, TX 78501
(956) 630-1499

San Antonio College of Medical and Dental Assistants
4205 San Pedro Avenue
San Antonio, TX 78212
(210) 733-0777

Southeastern Career Institute
5440 Harvest Hill, Suite 200
Dallas, TX 75320
(972) 385-1446

Kaplan Higher Education

Texas Careers
194 Gateway
Beaumont, TX 77701
(409) 833-2722

Texas Careers
6410 McPherson
Laredo, TX 78041
(956) 717-5909

Texas Careers
1015 Jackson Keller
San Antonio, TX 78213
(210) 308-8584

VIRGINIA

Dominion College
5372 Fallowater Lane, Suite B
Roanoke, VA 24014
(540) 776-8381

TESST College of Technology
6315 Bren Mar Drive
Alexandria, VA 22312
(703) 354-1005